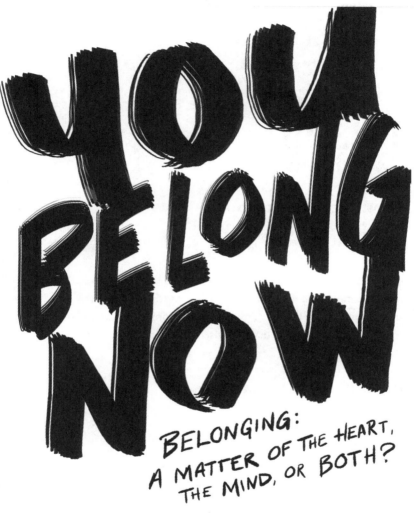

YOU BELONG NOW

BELONGING:
A MATTER OF THE HEART,
THE MIND, OR BOTH?

ED. D'AGOSTINO

www.mascotbooks.com

You Belong Now

©2020 Ed. D'Agostino. All Rights Reserved. No part of this publication may be reproduced, stored in a retrieval system or transmitted in any form by any means electronic, mechanical, or photocopying, recording or otherwise without the permission of the author.

For more information, please contact:
Mascot Books
620 Herndon Parkway, Suite 320
Herndon, VA 20170
info@mascotbooks.com

Library of Congress Control Number: 2019907678

CPSIA Code: PRV1219A
ISBN-13: 978-1-64543-041-4

Printed in the United States

"There is no greater agony than bearing an untold story inside you."
- Maya Angelou.

To my wife, Michelle; our children, Tim and Emily; our #2 son, Greg; and all others who helped ease the agony that lives inside of me by inspiring me to tell this story. My hope is that it challenges all people to live lives that show true acceptance and belonging so no one feels abandoned, forsaken, or forgotten ever again.

Introduction

What you will be reading in the pages of this book is neither only about me nor simply for me. Because of that, I am not going to be talking about myself in this introduction as so many authors seem to do in theirs—*"I wrote this for this reason or I wrote it for that," "I feel this way about this or I feel that way about that,"* and so on.

There once was a minister who used the word "I" so many times in his sermons that the people sitting in the congregation began to count them. It actually became a game of sorts with them: "Let's see how many times pastor will say the word 'I' in his sermon today," and they would keep count on their worship bulletins. So often in his messages there were phrases such as—"I believe this or I believe that, I think this or I think that…" and on and on and on it went. It actually got to the point where his messages became all about him and what he believed and thought, and people missed what he was actually trying to say to them. While it is good he had beliefs and thoughts, the point is he isn't the only one who believes things. He isn't the only one who thinks things. We all do. Every single one of us. However, when we lose sight of that, we become susceptible to getting lost in the quagmire of other people's thoughts and beliefs.

For far too long we have been a society caught up in the idea that, "I am more important than those who are strangers to me."

Or, "I am worth more...My opinions matter more...The life I live, the decisions I make, the responsibilities I face are more important than..." And while we cannot and must not lose sight of ourselves, we cannot and we must not lose sight of others either. And that is the reason for this story you are about to read. The words written here, the thoughts expressed, the emotions they trigger, and even the anger they may instill are for all of us, because in many ways all of us can and must relate to them in some way. For if you do not and instead simply dismiss these words as a "bullshit waste of my time," you will be doing yourself a disservice, because instead of allowing them to inspire and motivate you to fight for the freedom to grow and flourish as a united body, which includes all others, you will taste the defeat that comes from being selfishly disinterested, alone and fractured.

Did you ever hear the saying, "Likes repel and opposites attract"? Whether you have or have not, this saying still leads to the question: why is it different for humans? Why are we attracted to and only want to have some kind of relationship with those who are like us? Even opposite sexes. As an example, a husband wants his wife to like sports if he enjoys them, and if she doesn't he dismisses her interests as unimportant or worse. Or look how often a wife wants her husband to be more like her and enjoy what she likes. And when that doesn't happen their relationship is not nearly as close, divorce is justified with the excuse, "He wasn't like me," or "She never accepted me for me," and indifference forms. Yet I thought opposites attracted? So why would we want anyone else to be like we are, including our spouse? Aren't people more attractive when they are opposite? Why do we see those who are like us as acceptable and dismiss those who are different or foreign? Why do so many people consider the stranger to be nothing more than freakish and repellant?

CHAPTER 1

Albert Einstein once said, "A human being is part of a whole, called by us the Universe, a part limited in time and space. He experiences himself, his thoughts and feelings, as something separated from the rest a kind of optical delusion of his consciousness. This delusion is a kind of prison for us, restricting us to our personal desires and to affection for a few persons nearest us. Our task must be to free ourselves from this prison by widening our circle of compassion to embrace all living creatures and the whole of nature in its beauty."

In these words, Einstein is obviously talking about all living creatures, including those that are a part of the plant and animal kingdoms. However, at this moment in time, let us look at the living creatures referred to by us as humans.

How delusional is it to keep humanity separated into safely labeled categories, such as white, black, male, female, queer, or straight? And if you don't believe that mindset is delusional, that it is possible and even necessary to categorize humans, are you then saying what is delusional is to believe that all of humanity can live and work together as one compassionate, cohesive, smoothly running mechanism of change and growth, no matter who that person is or where they live? Anyone with half a brain knows the second option is more delusional than the first one, right? After all, how can strangers ever work together other than at their respective places of employment or during times of disaster? But as far as everyday living goes, how can you or I (or anyone else for that matter) accept and show someone compassion whom we've never met and know nothing about?

Take me as an example. I just did it again today. Someone whom I've never met was wearing a T-shirt with a slogan on it that I don't agree with. It actually made me very angry when I saw those words emblazoned across that man's chest, and yet here he was merely proclaiming to the masses a personal belief as he casually passed me on the street. But what did I do? Under my breath I muttered an assumption about the man that wasn't too nice. Then to make it worse, upon returning home I immediately went to social media and posted my displeasure of this stranger and denounced his narrow mindedness. This, regardless of the fact that I didn't and still don't know the man! I have never met him, nor have I had any kind of interaction or conversation with him, and yet I feel like I have every right to call his beliefs stupid and selfish even though he was innocently going about his day?

Denouncing and badmouthing others behind their backs is just so easy for me to do. I think there are times when I relish some kind of misplaced idea that I'm better than someone who doesn't agree with me and my ideas. Or I think about how much self-satisfaction I feel in making belittling or disparaging remarks about those whom I don't know. How I make them small in my mind so I can feel large, powerful, and all-knowing. And while I don't really have the guts to make degrading remarks to a person's face, boy oh boy, I sure don't have any problems making them under my breath, behind their backs or when I engage in gossip.

But yet isn't that selfish of me to do? And if it is selfish, then why do I do it? Why do so many of us? Could the reason be because devaluing others makes us feel superior to them in some perverted way? Do I think that I have so much more knowledge or information or I'm more in tune with current issues or whatever, so I truly believe I have every right to deflect my ego onto someone else? And is that what it is, ego? Am I egomaniacal in some way?

Regardless, no matter the reason, the question is where will my "better than thou" attitude get me in the end? Does that kind of attitude allow me to climb to some plane of success that I can only dream about right now? Or does my ego cause a measure of short-sightedness in me which results in my only looking at and seeing a narrow corridor of life and everything else that may enter my scope of vision, no matter how true or real, is worthless to me?

And yet thinking about it, why should I accept everyone else? Isn't that just dumb? Talk about an idiotic idea. I really think Einstein missed the mark on this one. Or did he...?

For as long as I can remember, music has been an important part of my life. When I say that, I'm not talking about making music. For you see, I was never one to be in a garage band, high school marching band, or any other kind of band for that matter. Truth is, I can't play an instrument or carry a tune to save my life. As a further detriment, the thought of being the source of another's amusement because of my less than adequate musical and vocal abilities, is just too much to bear.

Actually, one of the realities of my life is, as with most people and possibly even you, the thought of singing in front of others terrifies me. Because of this fear I choose to write words instead. Is it safer that way? For me, the answer is yes. Why? Because then I don't have to put myself "out there." I won't open myself up to embarrassment and failure, but can instead remain safely hidden behind the words that I write. And while it may be your opinion that hiding is the cowardly thing to do, in this case I don't think there is anything cowardly about it. Actually, it is my hope that by sharing my thoughts in a written form they will have some small measure of value that inspire those reading them in the same ways that I am inspired when I listen to music with the ultimate result being my words will be considered worthwhile and possibly even life-changing.

However, and putting aside my fear of singing in front of others, listening to music has always played a major role in my life. For you see, not only has listening to music been a source of joy and inspiration, it has also been a source of comfort to me. Why do I say that? Because in those moments of life where I find myself wallowing in the dark clouds of loss, defeat, or failure, listening to music, or singing to myself has this magical effect of giving me the strength to pull myself out of whatever funk I may find myself in so that I am more able to move forward. Music transports me to times and places of innocence where all feels safe and calm. And depending upon the song, music transports me to deeper, more inspired places in my thoughts and actions.

Is it the same for you? Do you enjoy listening to music or singing alone in the shower or car? Do the words or melodies from the songs you listen to speak to you in ways that inspire you to pull yourself out of a mire of blackness and see things in brighter ways? Does music transport you to better times and brighter days? To innocence and freedom? Does music reveal to you a depth of strength that lives inside of you that you'd otherwise be unaware of?

Being a middle-aged man, one of my favorite duos is The Carpenters. Throughout my life I've listened to their music countless times. Actually, at the age of 54 I still do, as this particular day attests. Because while I'm sitting here in my upstairs office putting these thoughts to paper, I am listening to their recording from 1970, "For All We Know." And as I listen to it, the words, "And love may grow for all we know…" begin to haunt me and I find myself turning away from what I am writing and asking myself the question: can love literally "grow?" And if it can, will it today?

Do I actually believe love can literally grow? If I, especially from the depths of my soul, believe that it can, then the answer must be yes. And if my answer is yes, then the next question that I must consider is, does that growth occur on its own or does love "depend" upon my help for real and sustained growth to happen? Actually, for its full growth to occur, does the emotion we call love need all of our help, working united, to bring it to life?

After all, we can, and often times do, profess love quite freely, don't we? "Love you…love you…love you…"

In like manner, how many of us know the Biblical words from 1 Corinthians 13 by heart? We see them written on plaques that are sold on the Internet, in gift shops and even department stores and I can safely say the words "Love bears all things, believes all things, hopes all things, endures all things…love never ends" are read at most weddings. Which leads to the question: do these words of love only have meaning in the moments when they are recited by those being married or as a nice sentiment scrawled across a plaque that hangs in our living room? Or must these words of love show active truth throughout all of life, no matter the situation, in order for verbally professed love to fully survive and grow in physically tangible and life-changing ways?

Does love truly "bear" all things and believe all things? For example, does the wife love the husband who physically, emotionally, or psychologically abuses her in any way? What if the wife does that to the husband? Do husbands and wives love each other unconditionally, no matter their circumstance? They may say they do, but do they act like they do? Does the husband truly love the wife he sees as more of a nag than any kind of life partner? Does the wife love the husband she sees as an incompetent, selfish child or irritation? Do they love each other and show each other support in times of financial, emotional, or health crises, or do they blame each other for the situation they find themselves in at that time of their lives and instead of love and hope, their words are filled with bitterness and anger? Why is it when all is good and easy, then the love they feel for each other is abundant and shared freely, but when all seems lost or hopeless, then thoughts and words take on accusatory tones such as, "It's because of you and your stupidity that we're in this mess, this is all your fault," and love is withheld or, worse, is nonexistent because it has purposely been replaced with harsh tones, disgust, and demeaning actions? And while I believe there are situations that require at least some measure of precaution to be exercised with them, allowing full blown restrictions to exist in showing and sharing love leaves no room to express it during the various situations, regardless if good or bad, that will undoubtedly present themselves to us throughout our lives.

Or how about kids? Do children love the parents who don't care about them or abuse them in any way, whether that abuse be physical, emotional, or worse, both? Do those same children believe or even feel they are loved for who they are? Do they feel as if they have value? And if they do, why? Why would they believe they are loved and how do they know it with any amount of certainty if professed love is not shown to them in real and affirming ways? Would I believe it if I found myself in any of those situations…?

CHAPTER 2

"If I have to come over there, I'm going to kill you, you little shithead," she yells at her daughter. "You never listen to me! What the hell is the matter with you? You act like some kind of spoiled brat! I didn't raise no spoiled brat, let me tell you, young lady! For the last time, get your ass over here and pick up this mess!"

Reluctantly the little girl walks over to where her mother is standing, knowing she is about to feel the sting of the back of her mom's hand across her little face. Why does her mom hate her so much? She sees how the other kids' moms are. Why does her mom have to be so different? Why is her mom angry with her all of the time? She tries really hard to behave and thinks she's doing a pretty good job of it, but the reality is her mother seems to have lost sight of the fact that she is just an eight-year-old girl. And being only eight, she is still learning and growing so she is going to make mistakes like everyone else, including adults like her mother and father.

"If you were never born I wouldn't be living in this hellhole!" her mother continues to yell. "It's because of you your father left and now I have nothin'! I try my best, the least you can do is show a little gratitude! But no, all you give a damn about is yourself! You're an ungrateful little bitch! He doesn't even come around here anymore! Why do you think that is, huh? And no, I don't think it's because of me."

"I'm sorry, Mommy, please don't hit me or yell at me anymore. Please. I'll try harder, I promise."

"Try harder my ass, you better not just try, you better figure out how to do better and do it already! Enough of this shit you've been pulling! I'm getting sick of it and sick of you!"

"I'm sorry, Mommy."

"Yeah, whatever. I'll believe it when I see it. Now clean up this mess. And enough of the boy games already! You're a little girl for god's sake!"

Ever since her father left, every day has been like this for her. Why can't her mom see her as she really is, a little girl who dreams of changing the world, or at the very least her own life…

Or how about beyond marital or parental love? What about those who feel the sting of injustice or discrimination? Do those who are discriminated against love those who advance a discriminatory mindset? Does the victim of discrimination give value to the discriminator and his or her feelings, opinions, or insights in any way, shape, or form?

And yet how does casual disregard, uncaring, or even abandonment show love? Isn't literally knowing, beyond any and all doubt, that he or she is loved, and as a result encouraged by others, the thing that gives someone hope to move forward even in the face of what appear to be impossible odds? After all, how can anyone truly encourage another if they don't have any kind of real and positive feelings for that person?

Or how about this question: does love exist everywhere? And if not, can it? Even between and among those who are strangers to each other?

While the possibility exists for emotional love to grow and never end, is it not true that without proper nurturing and expression, active love will not exist and will instead remain as nothing more than a feeling or hollow words from a song or poem? And if that is the case, does that not lead to the problem that if love remains nothing more than a feeling, where is the hope for humanitarian growth and acceptance in that mindset?

Actually, can we, as humans, fully grow without love and acceptance? Sure, we can say, "Absolutely, that would be no problem. I don't need everyone to love or accept me to go on living. Fact of the matter is, I don't need anybody."

Question is, how full is a life that includes love and acceptance compared to how limited and stifling is one's existence as a result of being unloved or not accepted?

And while you might say, "I am accepted by my circle of family and friends," how expansive or restrictive is that circle? Further, is it really good to be limited? While the proper answer may be yes in some areas, like speed limits or meal portions, how about in other areas of life, including love?

CHAPTER 3

Other words from the song include, "We've got a lifetime to share…" But does the lifetime we have to share include just future events that meet with our approval, or does that lifetime also include those future moments of doubt, frustration, and even disappointment that will inevitably occur? If we are honest with ourselves, I think we all know the answer to that question. Further, does not our lifetime also include the present moments we find ourselves in, as well as past moments that may have not only built us up but also hurt us or undercut our hopes and dreams? Past moments that have shaped and solidified who we are today and have helped to define how we see the world for tomorrow?

A further thought is who exactly are the "we" that each of us must include in the lifetime we've got to share? Only certain other individuals, like maybe those whom we may know or are related to, regardless if it be by blood or marriage? Should our lives only include those whom we feel closest to or who have done us some kind of favor? Or in order for love to fully exist as something more than just an emotion, must we accept the fact that we share life with everyone else, including those whom we may have never met nor will probably ever meet?

And if that's the case and we must include everyone in it, what would a universal love that fully exists look like anyway? Surely it would not be as intimate as the love shared between spouses or partners, or as strong as the love shared among and between family and friends, would it? There's no way it could be, is there?

Which leads to probably the most difficult question for anyone to answer concerning love: what does love between strangers really look like? How is it expressed when it is shared? Through the briefest passing glance on the street? Is that love between strangers? How about by simply asking them the question, "How are you?" Is that love between and among strangers? Of course not, those are just acknowledgements of another's presence, aren't they?

But this realization does lead to the real question on my mind, the question I can't help but ask myself: how do I show love, and not simple acknowledgment, to the stranger I am meeting for the first time or who crosses my path in some way? Because, as we all know, the reality is they are as much of a stranger to me as I am to them. So why should they care about my life and, in like manner, why should I care about theirs? Isn't it easier to just turn a blind eye toward another, to disregard them, to dismiss them as valueless? Aren't we taught that's the way life is meant to be? "It's a dog eat dog world out there and if you don't want to get eaten you better take the first bite."

"Supper'll be ready in about half an hour!" my wife Ann calls up the stairs to me.

"Okay, thanks!" I call back.

While I know it's early in the story I can't help but ask, are you at the point in this discourse where you are saying to yourself, "What kind of bullshit is this? Who wrote this piece of trash, some kind of 'libtard' or hippy freak with all of this love crap? Anyone with half a brain knows love doesn't exist everywhere and there's no possible way it could. Actually, it probably shouldn't anyway. Does this guy think that by asking all of these idiotic questions I'm suddenly going to have a change of heart and develop all of these warm fuzzy feelings which lead me to love all others in the world? Yeah right, like that's going to happen. Might as well throw this piece of trash in the garbage where it belongs." Any of these thoughts enter your mind?

If they haven't, good, let's keep moving forward. On the other hand, if they have, why do you feel loving others, including the stranger, is bullshit and only a love for those whom you know deserves to exist? And why do you feel it's only libtards or hippy freaks who have feelings of love and acceptance for all others and those of a 'sane mind' do not?

Regardless of your answer to either question, I humbly ask that you please keep reading. And as you read, please try to keep an open mind to receive the words written on these pages with an attitude of acceptance and not with the judgmental or dismissive mindset of "These are idiotic questions..." For if you allow yourself to be open to these questions concerning love and then carefully consider what your answers to those questions are, I truly believe you will find yourself experiencing a transformation of mind, which will lead to a transformation of heart, which will ultimately lead to a transformation of life. And not only for yourself, but for the world.

However, and while it may be my fondest of hopes that it will eventually happen, I don't expect some miraculous change of heart to instantly occur inside anyone reading this because of some random questions. Rather, my hope is that the questions I ask not only you, but also myself, will inspire each of us to look more deeply within ourselves to find that place where love not only exists, but has the opportunity to grow from.

Moving on with my thoughts and words, let's look at the Pilgrims for a moment.

"Hold on there one minute! Now what the hell is this guy talking about? First it was love, love, love; now he wants to talk about the Pilgrims? Is this guy on drugs or something? What do Pilgrims and love have to do with each other?"

Please bear with me and I believe you'll see where I'm going with this. Once again, and as an example, let's look at the Pilgrims. Do you think the Pilgrims loved each other when they first landed on this plot of ground we call the United States of America? And while your immediate response might be, "How the hell am I supposed to know, I wasn't on the boat with them," what happens to your response when you take into consideration what they accomplished together?

If you do that, I think you can safely say their unity was strong. It had to be. After all, imagine the journey they knowingly put themselves upon. They left everything they knew behind and united (which is the key factor in their story), embarking on a totally unfamiliar trek across an ocean. They had no idea what they would face, and not only on the journey but once they arrived, if they arrived at all. I mean, were they even sure they would make it to this new land? And that is why their unity is the key factor in their story. In order to successfully make that trip and transform an unknown territory into a thriving piece of land they could call home, they had to initially be united and accepting of each other. On top of that, we must also add that no matter the setbacks, hardships and failures they experienced in the formation of this country, they experienced them together. There was no room to blame each other for what they faced. They instead had to remain united in order to successfully overcome any and all obstacles to their united success and growth.

Question is, through their unity did some form of love exist between and among them? The initial answer could be yes; after all, we could argue they had to work together in order to continue to move forward with their hopes and plans and ultimately "make it" in their new home, didn't they? And in order to effectively work together they had to, at the very least, accept each other. There was no room for non-acceptance. They were all in the same boat, literally and figuratively. Every one of them found themselves surrounded by the new and the strange.

Then when we further take into consideration the fact that they left a familiar place, we come to the realization that the only thing that was familiar to them in this strange new land was each other. As such, they had no choice but to accept each other, different hopes, opinions, and all.

But do love and acceptance equate to the same thing, or are they two separate things entirely? After all, just because the Pilgrims accepted each other doesn't necessarily mean they loved each other, does it?

Or does it?

Is it simply that the love the Pilgrims had for each other was expressed in a form that is unrecognizable compared to the one that is so readily considered and accepted by adults in today's world?

The reason I say adults is because I think of how open and accepting of all others children are. Children have this amazing ability to see beyond race, gender, lifestyle, or belief and just openly welcome everyone else into their circle.

A wonderful depiction of this is Picasso's lithograph "The Youth Dancers, 1961." In this piece of art, Picasso shows a circle of figures holding hands dancing around a dove. The different colors that Picasso used in his depiction of the figures represent all of humanity uniting as one and the dove represents hope for peace among all people.

Now, while some of you reading this may be thinking to yourself, "So what, it's nothing more than just a picture," according to Picasso and I quote, "Art is a lie that makes us all realize truth." Which leads to the question, what is the truth we must come to realize, not only from this picture but maybe more importantly, from ourselves today?

Actually, one of those truths is there was at least one time in all of our lives when we were open to and accepting of all others; after all, every one of us began life as children, didn't we? We actually celebrated diversity and all of its beautiful nuances.

Studies have shown that all of us are born relational beings. That means that every human being, whether boy or girl, is born with an innate longing to be in relationship with others, regardless of who those others may be.

But when does all of that change? With the onset of adulthood? When being responsible to ourselves and those we know becomes more important than anything else in our lives?

Why is it as we grow into adulthood it becomes okay to discriminate against whomever we see as different? And please don't say, "That never happens..." because we all know it does. Is it because as adults we "know better" now and when we were children we were ignorant of professed 'man made' truths and instead fell victim to the 'fallacy' that all people are equal?

Why as children do we see others, no matter their age, gender, or race as equals and believe everyone belongs, but as adults we don't?

Or maybe better yet, especially for all of those reading this who know and influence children in any way, shape, or form, don't we actually teach our children to accept everyone..."Be nice to everyone in your class...Don't bully or insult any of the other kids...Watch what you say...Don't lie...No name calling...Don't be rude...Mind your manners...Be respectful...Keep your fingers to yourself..."

James Russell Lowell once said, "Children are God's Apostles, sent forth, day by day, to preach love and hope and peace." I believe children are the greatest gifts any and all societies could ever receive, and yet how many people in those societies, including the child's own parents, callously squander that gift through selfishly trying to make children miniature versions of themselves? Those who unquestioningly follow their parent's 'adult' beliefs or adopt their 'adult' mindsets no matter how narrow those 'adult' beliefs or mindsets may be?

I also believe we are called to celebrate our children and their unique and wonderful lives.

But how do we celebrate someone who goes against what we believe in and stand for, even when that someone is our own child?

Further, when we become adults, what happens to the gift society received through the acceptance we unselfishly showed others when we were children?

Why is it that just because we've become adults we now feel we have every right to only accept certain people into our circle of understanding and tolerance, and anyone who is not included in that circle is fair game to disregard and discriminate against?

As an example, all one needs to do is look at the past and current actions, as well as listen to past and current intolerant, judgmental, and discriminatory statements made by the leader of this country—a leader who was placed in office to represent everyone living in this country, not just those who believe what he believes and in the same way he believes them.

One of the biggest problems many are seeing, and actually speaking out about, is how this leader's words and actions, regardless of if they are fact or fiction, truth or lies, are merely shrugged off by many of his staunchest supporters as being acceptable; "Who cares what he says or does, we've elected him to the most powerful leadership position in the world even though he doesn't have any political experience. We support him no matter what he says or does."

Question is, why is that okay? What the hell happened? Or is it because these levels of discrimination and injustice have always existed, with the difference now being the everyday citizen, who has always believed in their necessity, now has a powerful spokesman to reignite them so that those actions and beliefs are once again seen as acceptable mindsets and behaviors, just as they were in past decades?

CHAPTER 4

"Need any help down there?" I yell to my wife.

"I'm fine, gonna start washing some of these dishes so there's not so many after supper!" she calls back.

"Okay, let me know when supper's ready!"

I was always taught that with age comes wisdom. But, and although I don't know if it's the same with you, for me it's not too wise to be intolerant and judgmental. Sure, it may appear to be safer that way, probably even feels safer that way, but is it really wiser? It is if our only goal is to live a life of selfish existence. And if that is the goal, then we can justify the wisdom and necessity of discrimination. However, I actually believe intolerance and judgment narrow our world because they lead to a level of unyielding discrimination which only serves to restrict our acceptance and understanding.

And what about today's world anyway? Why is it like it is today, even in this country? The existence of violence, racism, sexism, discrimination, intolerances, etc. is rampant. Again, I ask why? What happened?

Sure, some could easily say, "It's better than it was," while others might say, "It's always been this way...we've had discrimination for years...probably always will..." But just because there exists some level of belief that it's "always been this way," does that mean it has to stay this way, even today?

Actually, maybe the better question is why do we, as a people, continue to allow judgmental words and discriminatory actions to happen against other people? Has the world grown so large in population that the choice to disregard another, rather than try to understand their culture, traditions, religious beliefs, lifestyle, etc. and fully get to know them, is so much easier to make?

Even here in what we call the United States of America? Are we, the people of this country, so egocentric in our goal to self-fulfillment that someone else's goals are irrelevant because they are not the same as ours? How united are we becoming as opposed to how fractured are we growing every day?

Further, has social media—which proclaims to have made the world smaller—actually created a wedge that divides? After all, all one needs to do is consider the comments section of any online story or article. Is it not true they are, for the most part, filled with insights and opinions made by anonymous individuals with fabricated user names? Does social media not only allow us to remain anonymous, but at the exact same time openly share unjust, intolerant, hateful opinions of others all the while safely hiding behind the curtain of anonymity? And I don't know if it's just me or not, but it sure looks to me, from what I've read coming out of the mouths of others, that social media makes it easy to spread hatred.

But while most people would proclaim, "Social media is just another form of speech and we have freedom of speech," is it really freedom? After all, how free is someone who feels the need to cover themselves in a cloak of anonymity resulting from a fear of some unknown retribution or backlash?

But then again, what is freedom exactly, and where does it come from? Are we free because the law says we are? And if we say freedom is tied to laws passed by past governments, aren't we then enslaved to said government and the powers we personally attach to it? Thomas Jefferson once said, "A free people claim their rights as derived from the laws of nature and not as gift of their magistrate."

While we are called to stand united protecting our country and freedoms from any and all outside invasions, the sad fact is we are at war with each other inside our own borders. Howard Zinn stated, "Americans have been taught that their nation is civilized and humane. But, too often, U.S. actions have been uncivilized and inhumane." All one need do is to not only consider our past, but uncompromisingly witness the disregard and, at times, even hatred that has been and continues to be shown to so many members of American society today. Riots and protests and local wars and lashing out verbally and physically in uncivilized or barbaric ways seem to have become the norm. What is even sadder is that these behaviors appear to be done in the name of some self-absorbed mindset of, "I'm doing it for the betterment of all and love of country." As a result, the expression of one's self-absorbed mindset gives others permission to express their own selfish mindsets. And it appears it has gotten to the point where we are callously invading each other's privacy by allowing ourselves to be piloted down a road that leads to making it mandatory to produce personal information that was once considered sacrosanct in order to legally vote in a democracy.

Further, we crassly call each other names and foster feelings of us against them, even when the "them" are members of our own family or our next-door neighbors. We look with suspicion upon those who live, look, and believe differently than we do.

The crazy thing is, we are given even greater permission to engage in and foster these irrational behaviors by the actions of the leader of the free world. The man who represents every single one of us continues to stoop to the lowest level of engaging in them unhesitatingly. All anyone need do is look at his daily social media tweets. How often in those tweets does he devalue people he is supposed to lead in standing united as "low IQ crazy" while others he proclaims to be "psycho" or "nut jobs" and still others are "fake" or "fat" as well as all of the other insulting things he proudly and unreservedly says. His tweets are now to the point where he is inciting physical violence against the news media while proclaiming freedom of speech and freedom of the press. And that's okay? Really?

And while it is true some rush to his side proclaiming, "He's only defending himself against unwarranted attacks," the question is: are those who make this claim saying it's okay for the leader of the free world to verbalize and act in the same manner as those he professes are advancing fake information and exhibiting out of bounds behavior? The leader of the free world's lies, rants, and insults are fine? They are even justifiable? The president of the United States' words and behaviors are considered within the bounds of civility? Again, I must ask; really?

Another thing to consider about anonymity of social media: through it we don't have to form relationships. After all, there is no face to face dialogue, is there? We can say whatever we feel like saying when we feel like saying it, and with one click of a button we can turn it all off if we don't like what we read in response. How nice, how easy, how convenient, but yet how united is it making us and keeping us? Or, as I asked previously, and in spite of all of the good it has proven to do, does social media create a large wedge that divides us in real and selfish ways?

Thinking about it in some self-professed rational way, why should you or I, or anyone else for that matter, accept, respect, or even care about the rights of someone who doesn't have the same systems of beliefs, whether religious or political, that we staunchly profess to have?

Why should any one of us care about those who don't fit into our preconceived notions of what acceptance looks like and should look like? Ultimately, why should I put myself in the uncomfortable position of accepting someone I don't know? Would you? Do you?

Preconceived; now there's a loaded word. Defined as "an opinion formed beforehand without adequate evidence," the practice of preconception most likely leads to nothing more than a blanketed misunderstanding or judgment that encompasses an entire culture. All one need do is consider the following mindsets that exist: "Well you know all gays are…All Mexicans are…All Muslims are…All Republicans are…All Democrats are…All blacks or Hispanics or whites or whoever are…" This is a mindset that is allowed to live on and even grow to the point where preconceived notions have the final word, the upper hand, all of the power, when in reality the truth reveals quite a different scenario.

Again, look at the political landscape we find ourselves in. Again, look at the individual that was elected president of the United States of America. What are the messages this leader is sending to the people of this country and the larger world stage; anger, hatred, judgment, discrimination, selfishness? Or is he proclaiming messages of unity through selflessness, tolerance, and acceptance? Do his words invoke fear of or confidence in the stranger?

Or is it that the United States merely got its name because the physical land masses labeled states which encompass this country are simply united at their borders, and the complicated process of trying to get all of the people who live within the boundaries of said states to become and remain united, not only within but across said borders, doesn't need to be taken into consideration?

Ayn Rand once said, "Reason is not automatic. Those who deny it cannot be conquered by it." Is it reasonable to demand that our leaders provide us with some measure of assurance in not only the words they speak, but also in the actions they engage in? Or is that an unreasonable assumption, so we deny its importance and as a result can't be conquered by it?

After all, is it even fair to expect those in power to set the tone for the rest of us to follow? And yet, thinking about it and taking all factors into consideration, is it not true we are a society of followers? So, if those in power don't set the tone, who will? And if it is set by some unknown entity, how many of us would admittedly care and in the end unquestioningly follow the common stranger's example? As such, what tone is being set by those who are currently in power in your life, whether it is a boss, president, monarch, celebrity, or other business or world leader? Is their tone one of openness and understanding? Does their tone call for unity by showing those who experience it how to have mindsets of acceptance and welcoming?

Or does the tone that is being exhibited and shared contain an underlying feeling of selfishness, racism, and discrimination? And if we step back, truly examine all aspects and angles of said example, and we allow ourselves to simply follow it, the question then becomes: how can those accepting that negative mindset ever hope to advance if they allow their leader to actively show them, through his or her actions, they too have every right to condemn others in selfishly discriminatory and devaluing ways?

What is the message you are hearing and following today? The reason I ask that question is because it definitely appears there is a percentage of people living in this country that are embracing messages of anger and discrimination, zealously proclaiming them to be "just and fair, because we can finally get back on a track of healing after the last eight years of bullshit leadership."

And yet, it's one thing for any one of us to simply espouse love and acceptance; however, to actually demonstrate living that way is quite another matter. Saying, "I'm all for unity and will give it my best shot to make sure it happens..." but then to genuinely do whatever it is we need to do to make sure we live in unity are two very different things. Put the words into action, so to speak.

"Make the white man reign supreme and to hell with everyone else; they don't belong here, they need to stay in their own country."

"Those homo freaks don't deserve any rights."

"Build walls, not bridges."

"Kick their lazy good-for-nothing asses out of here."

"Let's go to war."

"It's okay to lie to people, tell them what they want to hear but then do the exact opposite."

"This might be the United States of America, but we don't have to remain united by accepting everyone."

Those are the messages that people are being handed, and look how many of them are eating up those proclamations in frighteningly ravenous ways? Question is, are you one of those people?

Or better yet, how many of those who greedily eat up messages instilling the virtues of non-acceptance proclaim "freedom for all" under some misguided loyalty to a mindset of "unless of course the 'all' includes those of a different race, gender, lifestyle, or creed?" If you hang onto any mindset that discriminates against another person, no matter who that person is, what they believe, or how they live, what real freedoms are you simply verbalizing that person deserves compared to asking yourself and then truthfully answering the question: how are your actions undermining as opposed to inspiring the words you speak?

CHAPTER 5

Then there's the verse from the song "For All We Know" that states, "So much to say…" After hearing these words, the valid question would be: what do we really have to say? How about to all others? Is it "so much" or is it very little? Are the words we speak to others commonplace and ordinary? Or are the words we say to others, including those people we may not know, uplifting and beneficial? Do the words we speak degrade, devalue, and fill another with self-doubt? Do our words undermine in any way? Are our words filled with love and understanding or are they words of judgment and condemnation brought about by the fear of the unknown, the strange, the preconceived, the unacceptable?

Further, how do the concepts of love and acceptance even work? After all, without first accepting "them" how could I ever possibly love another? How could anyone of us for that matter? Especially when we allow preconceived notions to rule the day?

Consider, no matter what I say, if I don't emotionally, psychologically, or physically accept someone into my circle of family or friends, how could I ever possibly have any kind of real conversation with them, get to know them and, as a result, have at least some small chance to love them? I couldn't. None of us could. There is no possible way that could ever truly happen, because through non-acceptance we keep them relegated to that safe identity known as stranger, including those we proclaim to be family.

Consider, if someone in our "inner circle" is different and we do not fully accept that difference and do not truly get to know all aspects of their personality and life, what we are doing is keeping a very large part of that person a stranger. And if we can so easily do that to a family member or proclaimed friend and justify our non-acceptance of them because of this, that, or the other thing, what in the world is there to stop us from doing the very same thing to a stranger? We all know there isn't anything. As a result, isn't it much easier to ignore the plight of the stranger compared to those whom we accept as family?

My grandmother used to say, "It's a dangerous business giving your heart away." As I said before, we could very easily say the words "I love you." However, no matter how many times we speak those words if we don't 'give our hearts away' in some tangible form and actively express the emotion that must live behind our proclamations of love, the truth is "I love you" will exist as nothing more than three words. Three words that so easily fall from our mouths or are so easily written across the page. And if that's the case then what are we truly saying in those three words? Is it so very much or is it so very little?

And what actually ties those words to, and ultimately turns them into, action so that the love that supposedly lives behind them does not simply remain an emotion scrawled across the page of some obscure volume of poetry, randomly quoted from some song or passage of scripture or sentimentalized in a greeting card, but becomes real and life-changing in that it does away with any easy preconception?

After all, when we add the idea of preconception, more likely than not we find ourselves generalizing. Which I guess every one of us can safely say we do in one way or another, at many times and in many ways. The thing we must remember is, just because we can and so often do generalize, while it might make many situations easier to face, generalizing doesn't always make the situation right, does it? Besides, generalizing is not needed in order for someone to enjoy true, and not just fake or preconceived, fullness of life, is it?

After all, how productive, how loving, is it to generalize? While it is true it may feel empowering to do so, the reality is generalization is something that is quite dangerous for any one of us to allow ourselves to engage in. Why? Because generalization leads to judgment, which leads to misunderstanding, which leads to frustration and ultimately, anger. And what develops out of anger? Dissension, hatred, selfishness, preconception, and non-acceptance. As a result, where in all of that negativity does real love exist between the peoples of the world? However, without allowing generalized preconceptions to rule our hearts or mindsets, doesn't love have a better chance of existing among and between all?

Or maybe our expression of love depends upon how we are loved by others. Think about it; if we feel like no one likes, let alone loves, us are we going to be fully open and receptive to another or are we going to close ourselves off in some manner so that we can feel even a small measure of safety against the storm of those things that make us doubt and question the value of who we are?

Or is our assessment of the value of love only determined by how we personally define it? Does having love for another only mean having this "I'd die for you at any cost" feeling, or must the emotion of love include subtler and less extreme expressions and not only those that we define in preconceived concrete terms? Which expression of love leads to the better way? Which expression of love leads to full and faithful acceptance and which one limits those possibilities?

The questions are so hard to answer, so hard to face. But it would appear that face them I must. Especially when I look at the world and what is happening in it today. For example, there are the issues of homelessness, hunger, injustice. How often have I heard others speaking out so vehemently against the legalization of same gender marriage? Or look at the continued gun violence that exists or the blatant expression of discrimination justified by politics or religious beliefs and on and on. Look at all of the ugly things we do or say against others every day. Things that are so commonplace and ordinary we don't even think about them, nor the consequences that result; and that's just in this country. The issues of lovelessness existing throughout the entire world can seem too overwhelming to even think about. But yet, if I turn a blind eye toward questions concerning love, as it would appear so much of society is doing and continues to do, am I not then just as guilty as so many others of selfishness and self-absorption? If I only care about the current mindset of self-comfort or personal opinion, and do not challenge those selfish mindsets and opinions in order to look in broader and more progressive ways, am I doing all that I need to be doing to demonstrate love?

So often I have heard people making the generalized statement, "The world is going to hell in a handbasket." My question is what is their basis for making that statement? What justifies that belief? Why do so many people believe that the "world" is going to hell in a handbasket? Has everyone who makes that statement seen the whole world? Have they experienced all cultures across the globe? Do they understand the makeup of other people's lives around the world? Or is that generalized statement a preconception?

Just because they believe the world is going to hell in a handbasket as a result of some generalized preconception that all people of a different nationality are this and all of those "perverted deviants" who live that lifestyle are that, and anyone with such a "psychopathic belief in sky fairies" most assuredly is...does that make it the truth for the rest of the world, including you or me? Or is the idea that "the world is going to hell in a handbasket" simply their personal truth encompassing their personal world? And if it is their personal truth, which I unconditionally accept and respect, then why denounce, disrespect, or devalue me for my personal opinion(s) and, as a result, try to force or guilt me into making their opinion my truth? Why is it so easy to judge me if I don't believe something or feel the same way as they do about an issue?

After all, if I simply allow the opinions of society to influence and guide me so that I feel like an accepted part of said society, what then happens to me? Am I all that I can possibly be? Do my personal viewpoints carry any weight, or is it only my agreeing with the thoughts, opinions, and viewpoints of others all that matters? Do I allow the question, "What happens if I don't believe the same thing as they do," live and grow in me until I ultimately lose sight of who I am for fear of what others may say about me or think of me?

Because what will happen if I don't believe the "whole world" is going to hell in a handbasket? What if I don't believe that all homosexuals are evil deviants out to prey upon weak and innocent children or all Muslims are hell-bent on murder and destruction or all Democrats are liberal idiots or all Republicans are tight-assed Bible-thumping, judgmental "know-it-all's…Would I then be conceived as an enigma? Would I be something generalized as unacceptable by a certain segment of the population?

If the answer is yes, then the question I must face and ultimately answer is: can I live with that? Can any one of us for that matter? Or has acceptance and belonging to something larger than just some narrow circle of personal beliefs become so important in today's society that conformity carries more weight than truth, even if that acceptance means selling myself out?

Actually, if it does and as a result I just simply conform to the ways of society, what is society ultimately getting from me in the end; the truth of who I am and what I truly believe or a misconception based upon some self-imposed or societally advanced preconceived and generalized idea of the value of conformity that I am so desperately trying to fit in with?

CHAPTER 6

"Ow!"

"What happened?" I call to my wife.

"Oh, stupid me, I cut myself with a knife doing the dishes," she calls back.

I quickly get up from my desk and run down the stairs to see. The questions about love, acceptance, and preconception will have to wait.

"Are you all right?"

"Look at me, look at all of this blood, how can you ask me such a stupid question? Ow, that hurts. Of course, I'm not all right."

In hindsight, I guess it was a stupid question. But like almost everyone else, it's the first thing that pops into my head. How many times have I asked someone who is hurt that question? Or better yet, how many times have I told someone, "It will be all right, you'll be fine…" even though I could see the true reality of the situation, albeit the injury be either physical or emotional. Do you or I, or any others of us for that matter, say the words, "You'll be all right" to make ourselves feel better; to solidify in our own minds the hope that no matter how bad things look, the other person will be all right in the end? Is that because if we believe they are all right, then we can have peace of mind?

What about the homeless, what about the hungry, what about the unaccepted, those who feel the sting of discrimination and injustice in any way, shape, or form; are they all right? And just because we believe they are, are they really? Do we tell ourselves those, for example, who are homeless are where they are because of the choices they've made in life? Does that make it easier for us to ignore their plight?

"It's their own fault..."

"Lazy good-for-nothing..."

"They're the ones who choose to live, act like, or...so why should I worry about them?"

Right?

After all, isn't the proper mindset, the proper response to those who are strangers, "Why should I care about them?" And really, why should we care about them? After all, do they truly care about us? They may say they do with words, but what about through their actions? What message are people's actions sending? And just because that is a small segment of the population's actions, or should I say inactions, is it all right to make it all-encompassing over the whole of humanity?

"Let's get you to the emergency room, that cut looks serious."

"I'm not going to any emergency room and my mind is made up, so just get that idea out of your head right now! Good Lord, just give it a minute, it'll stop bleeding. I'll be fine, Mr. Worrywart."

Even though I know the cut won't stop bleeding, again looking at the wound, I figure I'll humor my wife, not press the issue, and just help her as best as I can.

"Let's get that cut washed out. We'll need to bandage it for you. Do we have any antibiotic cream to put on it? Let's see what we have here. Doesn't look so bad."

I try to sound reassuring, but I fear I'm failing miserably for I can see the truth of just how bad her cut is and I'm sure that truth is coming through in my voice. I hope not, but I wouldn't count on it.

After seeing the depth of the cut, there is no doubt in my mind my wife is going to need stitches. Regardless, I do my best to ease her pain and tend to the wound on her hand. But alas, it isn't enough.

Twenty minutes later, after having changed my wife's bandage twice and her mindset once, we are in the car racing to the emergency room of the nearest hospital, which is still forty minutes away. The bleeding has not let up; in fact, it seems to have gotten worse, much like my wife's humor.

"Life is nothing but a bunch of shit," my wife proclaims.

"Excuse me?

"You heard me. Life is lousy."

"Why would you say that?" I ask her.

"Just look at our lives. Look at us. Here we are, struggling every single day. And now this, I cut my hand; how much do you think this will cost us? I'm sure insurance won't cover it all. So, add to the struggle. Life is just so much fun, isn't it? And look where your job has us: stuck in the middle of nowhere. Have to drive an hour one way to get to anything, even the hospital, if that's what you want to call it."

While it is true I had been there a number of times to visit patients, I wouldn't call where we are headed to a hospital. I would say it is more like a "stop-over." What I mean by this is, while by all appearances it looks like a hospital, with doctors and nurses and staff running around pushing gurneys or carts of medicine, according to the locals, if one is sent there the best thing they can do for themselves would be to get transferred to a place that provides better care. As a matter of fact, it has such a bad reputation it is actually referred to by many as "a dog house." According to most people who have gone there, the medical staff is inferior, the food is terrible, and the rate of misdiagnosis is actually quite frightening. But my wife needs stitches in her hand, and I am not capable of fulfilling that need. Besides, I reason, how hard can it be for trained medical professionals to stitch my wife's wound; it's not like its brain surgery. We'll be in and out in no time, I tell myself.

But on top of my wife's physical wound there are the emotional wounds, caused by what truly has been a difficult life, that I must also consider. How do I respond to my wife's insights about our life that takes her emotional wounds into account and gives them the value they deserve? After all, emotional wounds can't just be sewn up and bandaged, then in a few days or weeks they'll be completely healed and all will be fine with the world. I believe that every single one of us has suffered emotional wounds in some way, shape, or form. As such, we all know firsthand how deep emotional wounds live in our lives. Emotional wounds can go right to the heart of our soul and take up residence there if we allow them to. And it seems this is exactly what my wife has allowed hers to do.

CHAPTER 7

The snow was coming down pretty steadily that day, and being trapped indoors created a mood of warmth and safety for Ann. The bland ordinariness of her surroundings took on a new excitement because of the fact that school was canceled due to the weather, and that cancellation opened the doors to all sorts of possibilities for her.

The one thing she loved to do more than anything else was draw pictures, for in them she found a whole new world of wonder and excitement that she alone created and had total control over. Hm, control, now that was something that was sorely lacking in Ann's life. Actually, the lives of her entire family. Every day her parents seemed to be filled with doubt and worry and that caused her to feel uneasy. The way they argued so often, especially over money, made her feel like she was nothing more than some worthless piece of baggage that only caused more heartache and stress in their lives. Yes, maybe she could draw all day. That would be awesome. Leave the smallness of her life behind and find some grand utopia in the creation of an amazing fantasy landscape filled with color and magic. *That's what I'll do, I'll draw today*, Ann told herself.

But isn't drawing stupid? Isn't it a waste of time? That's what she was told by so many others, at least the adults in her life, including her parents, relatives, and even teachers. And because of that, the voices in her mind played over and over and over and as a result, the only things she could hear were the endless comments and questions which caused so much doubt and discomfort for her. Where is the future in drawing silly pictures? You can't pay the bills drawing. You need something else to get a good job and live your life in comfort, not just drawing stupid pictures. On and on went the negative comments by those who Ann thought were supposed to support her the most.

Up to this point, life had not been easy for Ann. And it didn't look like it was going to get any better. Once again, her father was out of work and she could feel the tension growing daily between her parents. She heard their daily arguments: "Where are we going to get the money for this? How are we going to pay for that bill? If only I would have gone to college, I could have gotten a better job and we wouldn't have to worry all of the time. Aren't you sick and tired of worrying all of the time, because I know I am."

By the same token, her mother was always trying to sooth the wounds that seemed to cut the family in half: "Please try to stop worrying so much, we'll be all right. Money isn't everything you know, at least we have each other. If I have to, I'll find a job and help us out financially. You're not going through this alone, none of us are. We're all in this together and together we'll get through it. Please try to have a little hope."

"Hope for what, that this will stop?" her father countered. "Sorry, but I don't see it stopping. Hell, if it's been this bad for this long, I don't think it's going to be getting any easier any time soon. Why should I have hope in two failures like us? Besides, who would hire an old fart like me? Nobody, that's who. All companies want are these young kids just getting out of school so they don't have to pay them much and they can train them to be the way they want them to be..."

Why couldn't the arguments just stop already? Why did there always have to be so much tension? Life isn't supposed to be this hard, but adults make it hard with their constant worrying and fighting. Why aren't things easier? Ann no longer felt like drawing. Life once again had taken the hope away and filled her mind with questions that denounced and degraded. Why create some kind of stupid escape that doesn't and never would exist? Why waste the time? Apply yourself more to reality and let the fantasy stuff by the wayside. No one cares about that anyway, so why should you?

And instead of continuing to see the beauty of the snow, now all Ann saw was a mess that was cold and uncomfortable. There was no escaping it. Why bother trying to anyway? Use your energy for something more useful, Ann. Something that will make others proud of you.

Unfortunately, no matter how much Ann told herself she could escape this life she now found herself living in, deep down she felt the sting of failure. She knew firsthand the doubts and despairs that eat away at you until all that is left is bitterness and envy. Envy for something and someone who seems to have it better than you think you'll ever have it, no matter the sacrifices you make. Ann knew first-hand how those who are supposed to encourage you the most merely degrade and devalue any and all dreams you may have for yourself, especially if those dreams don't line up with their mindset or definition of success. Or is it because they didn't have any dreams for themselves? Did the "ugliness" of their reality take away the beauty of dreams? And in the end, Ann came to the belief that if no one else believed in her, not even her parents, why should she have faith in herself?

And as I discovered when I met her, it was that way throughout all of Ann's life. How often has she shared with me the many moments of hope and faith that were quickly turned into times of doubt and despair? How often has she shed tears because any semblance of happiness was squashed by attitudes and mindsets of 'woe is me' by her parents and the other adults who lived in her hometown? It was like they were all surrounded by this thick veil of defeat and no one had the desire to try to tear it down. Rather, it was like everyone who existed there had settled into this mindset of, "Oh well, that's just the way it is and has always been. Nothin' we can do about it anyway, so why try to change it?" Who would have any chance of finding and maintaining any semblance of hope against that barrage of negativity? I'm sure it wouldn't be too many. Wounds would be cut too deep and, as a result, the scars that remained would be a constant and relentless proclamation of doom.

And while I had the privilege to share in Ann's moments of bravado and positivity, they were short-lived and ended up becoming decimated completely that day five years ago. A day that resulted in her withdrawing into herself and created what those who don't really know her would readily label an unfeeling attitude. However, what others may see as nothing more than selfishness or blissful arrogance, I know as a mask of courage she wears in order to hide the pain and self-doubt that eat at her for so many moments every day of her life.

CHAPTER 8

To add to my dilemma, because my wife's humor definitely is not the best, I know if I say one thing, the response will be a negative comeback, and yet if I say a different thing, the response will still be a negative comeback. Possibly even more negative. So, what do I say to her, how do I comfort her in these moments of anger, pain, and doubt? What is it that I am supposed to say? I feel like I'm in a no-win situation. Like, as the proverbial saying goes, I'm stuck between a rock and a hard place. As a result of my dilemma, I don't say anything, which I know will lead to even more confrontation.

"So, no comment? Well, I guess I know how you feel about all of this. 'Keep your mouth shut' right? 'All you do is complain.' Right?"

I feel like I'm drowning, the waves of hopelessness washing over me, pulling me further and further down. All I want to do is get her to the hospital. I try to convince myself maybe once her cut is stitched then her mood will lighten, but I know the truth. And it's a truth I have no desire to face at this moment.

"I never said, 'All you do is complain.'"

"You might not have said it, but I'm sure you thought it."

"How do you know what I'm thinking? Right now, all I'm thinking about is getting you to the hospital and getting that cut looked at."

"Yeah, right, that's all you're thinking about. Why don't you ever tell me the truth?"

"What do you mean I never tell you the truth?" Funny, here I am, right back where I left off before my wife cut her hand. Wondering about truth in love and now she is asking me why I never tell her the truth. Don't I? Do I hide the truth from my wife in some way? Is she right and I should start being more truthful? But I thought I was truthful with her. Some days this is just so hard, Lord. Like this very moment, trying to concentrate on the road, worrying about my wife, the cut on her hand, and now this to add to it, God help me, why is this so hard?

Turning to my wife, I say to her, "I'm always truthful with you."

"What do you mean you're always truthful with me? How can you say such garbage?" she responds. "And keep your eyes on the road!"

"Why do you call it garbage?" Her mood is definitely getting worse and it isn't doing much to improve mine. As a matter fact, I can feel myself getting more and more stressed with each passing mile. Why aren't we at that hospital yet? God, this is taking forever, I think to myself.

"It's garbage because what value do your words have?"

"Now what is that supposed to mean?" I ask her.

"Look how much value the people you preach to place on your words. The way I see it, not much has changed in the mindset of all of those good 'church folk.' They still look like the same 'stuck in tradition' group to me. I listen to your sermons, trying to challenge them to think beyond their preconceived notions of things, look at the bigger picture, try new ways of doing things. But has anything changed? The way I see it, no. All I see is how they just sit in their pews, and I emphasis *their* pews, like they know what's right and what's wrong, judging everybody else who looks or thinks or lives differently than they do.

"Then," she continues, "they hide behind their religion and justify their so-called righteous opinions by proclaiming other people's actions and behaviors are sins against God. Well aren't they sinning by being judgmental? Doesn't the Bible say, 'Judge not lest ye be judged?' But they go right on judging, don't they? So that tells me they are knowingly sinning, and they're okay with that. To me, the real measure of a Christian isn't how many times they're sitting in church but how closely they're living their lives according to the teachings of Christ outside of the church. After all, God doesn't just live in some building, does He?"

She goes on, "Or how about when you were first appointed here, remember how many people told us, 'If you weren't born in this town, you'll never be accepted by these people'? Boy, this cut hurts. They sure were right, weren't they?

"And you know how they bitch, complain, and talk about you behind your back. Look how they talk about us. Hell, look how they talk about each other. Don't they realize other people hear them? And a lot of those people are outside of the church.

"Or how about when we first got here; remember what that one faithful man of God said to someone, 'What do you think of that yahoo preacher they sent us?' Yahoo preacher? What right does that 'good Christian' have calling you or anyone else they don't know a yahoo? Who the hell does he think he is anyway, God almighty, that he feels he has the right to belittle before he even gets a chance to know you?"

Immediately I think to myself, "Back to the idea of preconception." But no matter what I'm thinking; my wife's tirade continues.

"Good man of God, let me tell you. And what's worse, if you ever asked him why he called you a yahoo, you know what his answer would be: 'I never said that.' Hell, if we ever asked any one of them why they talk about this one or that one, or us, you know all of those good Christians would pretend innocence and deny they ever said or did any of it. Or they'd say those 'kind of' people are sinful heathens. That makes the church look really good doesn't it; a place filled with gossiping hypocrites. I don't know how you can minister to these people when you know first-hand how judgmental and condemning they are."

Trying to change the subject, I ask her, "How does the bleeding look; can you tell if it's let up any?"

"Doesn't look like it has. But the way you have it wrapped I can't even see my own hand, so how the hell am I supposed to know?" I guess now she's saying I didn't wrap the cut on her hand to her liking. God, this is taking forever.

"Now where did all of this come from?" I ask her.

"Where did all of what come from; my mood, my attitude? Where do you think?"

"You are upset because of your cut, which is understandable. But this idea that people in the church don't listen to me?" It's funny, but it seems like every one of our conversations goes right back to the church and the people in it. It's like we wouldn't have anything to discuss if we weren't talking about church issues. "Some of them listen to what I'm saying; look at how good they work together. True, not everyone is going to want to hear what I have to say, but name me one person who everyone listens to. Does everyone listen to you? No, of course they don't. That's the way it is in life."

"Yeah, well, maybe, but just because that's the way it is in life right now, does that make it okay to keep it that way? Or what about those who don't like you in the church and just up and leave the place; what do you think they have to say about you? Good things? Actually, I'm sure you have a pretty good idea what they are saying, and not only with words but with actions, and those words and actions aren't very Christian, let me tell you. How do you think their attitudes are affecting their God? Think they're making Him proud? Just because they personally don't like what you have to say doesn't give any one of them the right to go around badmouthing you. All they are doing is turning more and more people away from the church. But they're too blind or stupid or whatever you want to call it to realize it. Actually, selfish might be the better word."

"Why do you say they are selfish?" I ask her.

"I say they're selfish because look at what happens when the church isn't being run the way they like or think it should be run. Like for example, worship music. If they don't like the way the worship music is, such as the use of a piano versus an organ, instead of swallowing their pride, sticking around, and showing the other people there their support of it, what do they do? They get their asses in the air and they selfishly take their toys and go home. Their attitudes are like spoiled kids. They act like if they can't 'play with the blue truck,' they aren't playing. What does that say about those 'good Christian church folk?' To me and so many others it shows the true reasons they are in church in the first place; to gossip and for the preacher. And if they don't like the preacher, then 'the hell with it, I'm not going back until he or she is gone.' My question is, where does their precious God fit into the mix if those are their narrow-minded attitudes? Ever ask yourself that question? It's like they aren't in church to worship God as much as to keep tabs on the preacher, and if they don't like what they see or hear, *adios amigos*. And you can't tell me it's not. But hey, you're the minister, you have a better understanding of this than most people. You're the one on the front lines facing it every day, so how do you see it? But before you answer, let me ask you: how do you think the rest of the world sees it and what do you think it will take to change that perception?"

"I don't know; right now, all I'm concerned about is you and getting that cut looked at by someone who can help you. I'm not thinking about all of that other stuff. There are more important things to worry about right now, so just put those thoughts out of your mind," I say in response.

"Sure, I figured as much, avoid the question. You know, I see the way all of these 'good church folk' are acting and I'm beginning to understand more and more why so many people are saying churches are filled with nothing but hypocrites. Good Lord, just look how they acted when the Supreme Court legalized same gender marriage. It was like it was the end of the world. But is that what happened? No, of course not. The USA did not come to an end. The world did not stop spinning. Instead, what happened, things went on as usual for them, that's what. While it is true the Supreme Court's ruling on the legalization of same-sex marriage is of significant historical importance, it did not take away anyone's right to marry whom they love, did it? What it actually took away was the prejudice surrounding an issue that personally affects good church folk how?"

My wife is on a roll as she continues, "While the idea of a same gender couple marrying might be an abominable idea to many church folk, while it may go against their Christian beliefs and biblical teachings and understanding, how did the Supreme Court's ruling prejudice a follower of Christ's personal beliefs in any way? How did it stop them from believing how or what they want and even need to believe? In actuality, the ruling didn't take away any of the thunder of their belief. It's still as strong today as it was yesterday and will be tomorrow, isn't it?"

She goes on to say, "Being a true follower of Christ certainly doesn't mean I abandon my principles or you simply move to my side of the issue that divides us, does it? Being a true follower of Christ means recognizing, understanding, and showing the love He taught by truly celebrating the diversity that exists all around us. Isn't it supposed to be that the church is not about being strong enough to use judgment—rather, it's about being strong enough not to? Don't you preach that as His followers we must believe that all are equal in the eyes of God? Or are some people nobodies in God's eyes and others are somebodies? Are His rules that restrictive, or did He change the rules Himself with the new covenant He sent in the birth of His Son Jesus who brought a new command that supersedes all the laws and the prophets—the new command to love as you want to be loved?"

"You know He brought a new covenant of love," I respond.

"Then why is it so easy for so many of them to go around spouting 'Love thy neighbor, love thy neighbor...' but boy oh boy, they sure don't hesitate to show hatred and judgment against the neighbors who go against their precious beliefs. I mean, what if their neighbors are gay or Muslim, or on welfare and drugs? Would they love them, or is their definition of 'love thy neighbor' narrowly confined to a 'chosen few?'" my wife asks.

A very valid question, I think to myself. What if the neighbor is LGBT? According to the Bible, that kind of behavior is an abomination in God's eyes. But as true and faithful believers living in today's world, and I emphasis the words 'today's world,' must it be an abomination in our eyes as well? As one woman just recently put it concerning same sex marriage, "It's just down right wrong, it says so right in the Bible." She speaks with such conviction, such finality, that I'm not sure how to respond. Especially in a way that will honor and not challenge her belief.

Or is it time for her and so many others like her to be challenged? Because if their beliefs are not challenged, what will happen to not only the church, but possibly the country as a whole, I ask myself.

Another thought enters my mind: was the world that Christ walked upon progressive and forward-thinking, or was it stilted and backward-focused?

"Or how about religious freedom," my wife continues. "They proclaim, 'Religious freedom for all because this country was founded on religious freedom.' Well what about Muslims or Buddhists? Those, along with how many other faiths, are recognized religions in this country, aren't they? So, don't those who practice them deserve to enjoy the protection of religious freedom too? It is no wonder so many people bring up the issue of hypocrisy, the way Christians gossip and act. Their attitudes and actions aren't doing much to show others they've learned the lessons of peace and love taught by the one they proclaim to worship and follow. They sure aren't doing much for my spiritual well-being, I'll tell you that. God, this cut hurts. Aren't we soon there? Any other time you drive like a maniac and now you're doing the speed limit. I'm sure if it was one of your precious parishioners the situation would be different, but who cares about me, right?"

"Boy, you are in a mood."

"Of course, I'm in a mood—I've been in this mood for quite some time, only you're too blind to see it. Caught up in your good pastor role; trying to keep everyone happy, including the conference that shit on you. Everyone, that is, except you and your family. And please don't tell me you're happy. I've seen how all of this nonsense is affecting you. Why should you be happy anyway, after how the conference discriminated against you because you have epilepsy? Telling you they didn't know what to do with you. Telling you they couldn't keep making accommodations for those with disabilities, yet you never asked them for one single accommodation. Even your clergy mentor told you he would have left long ago, but no, you stick around; for what, I'd like to know. Did it advance your career in the church in any way? Did it help us in any way? Far as I can see, no. Like I said, all the conference did was shit on us. Use your epilepsy against you. Remember that conversation? I'll never forget it, you came home from that meeting like a whipped dog."

Ed. D'Agostino

CHAPTER 9

Even though it happened over eight years ago, the sting of discrimination still felt like it was yesterday.

"Hello! Yes, this is Todd. Oh, hi Martin, how are you doing? What's that? You want to meet with me and Evelyn from BoOM in your office tomorrow at 3:00 p.m.? Sure, that's no problem, I'll see both of you then. Take care. Bye."

"Who was that?" my wife asks.

"My District Superintendent, Martin. He wants to meet with me tomorrow in his office."

"What's going on?"

"I don't know, I didn't ask him. All he said was Evelyn from the Board of Ordained Ministry wants to meet with him and me in his office at 3:00. I suppose it has something to do with my interview with BoOM and ordination, but who knows for sure. Try not to worry about it, it'll be fine. Remember, these are people of God after all…"

That night I couldn't sleep. Instead, I lay awake tossing and turning, wondering what tomorrow's meeting would bring. I thought the interviews went well, but did I miss something? I must have screwed up somehow, but how? God, I'm nothing but a failure. What did I do wrong? Was it something I said? Was it something I didn't say?

After what turned into one of the longest nights of my life, I definitely never expected to hear what I heard in that meeting from a church conference representative...

"Good afternoon, Todd. Won't you come in."

"Apologies I'm a few minutes late, so what's up? Why did you want to see me?"

"Evelyn wanted to talk to us about your interview with The Board of Ordained Ministry yesterday. Apparently, they have some concerns."

"Hello, Evelyn, what concerns do you have and how can I help alleviate them?"

"Your interview with BoOM went fine, but there's one thing that prevents us from ordaining you."

"Oh really, and what would that be?"

"We don't know what to do with you."

"Excuse me?"

"The Conference's and BoOM's greatest concern is we don't know what to do with you."

"What do you mean you 'don't know what to do with me'?"

"You told several people in the conference that you suffer from epilepsy, correct?"

"Yes, that is correct."

"You also said this epilepsy causes you to forget things, right?"

"Yes, when I have a seizure, one of the side effects is short term memory loss. But I don't see why that is concerning you to the point of preventing you from ordaining me. I do my job and I do it well. Everything this conference has asked me to do I've done and more. I've never received one complaint from anyone here, have I, Martin? You don't have any problems with my work, do you?"

"No, I don't. I would say you are one of our best ministers. Your paperwork is always submitted to the office on time and in order and the people of the churches you serve speak well of you. I haven't heard one complaint," replied Martin.

"So, what does my suffering from epilepsy and memory loss have to do with ordaining me?" I asked Evelyn.

"Like I said, we don't know what to do with you. I mean, what if we ordain you and appoint you and you have a seizure and can't remember something. What are we supposed to do with you then? You know how it works in this denomination, once you're ordained, you're guaranteed an appointment to a church. You'd have a seizure, have memory loss, you'd be ordained, and we'd be stuck with you. So, we're very hesitant to ordain you because, like I said, we don't know what to do with you. You can see our dilemma, can't you?"

"I can't believe you're sitting here saying you don't know what to do with me and that you'd be stuck with me! Like I'm some kind of disease or something."

"I'm sorry for being so blunt. Of course, I don't mean you're a disease. But what would you do if you were in our position? Surely you can see the difficult position we find ourselves in?"

"So, you say you don't know what to do with me and you're stuck with me. Could you give me an example of what you mean by my memory loss affecting my ministry?"

"Sure; suppose the sister of the woman whose husband you buried a week ago calls you and says, 'Hi, this is so-and-so, do you remember me? You buried my sister's husband last week…' and because of the epilepsy you don't remember her, what are you going to say?"

"I'd probably say 'hello,' repeat her name, and ask her how she is doing after the loss of her brother-in-law. Wouldn't that be the proper way to handle it? Isn't that how you would handle it?"

"First of all, this has nothing to do with me and how I'd handle the situation. Second, no matter how you handle it in this case, what do we do in the future if it keeps happening over and over again, your memory issues? We just don't know what to do with you. Actually, we're not sure if you even belong in ministry, let alone this conference."

"What do you mean you don't know if I belong in ministry, let alone this conference?"

"The conference is all about making sure that the right ministers are placed in the right church setting to lead more and more people to Christ, and with your memory loss issues, we're just not sure if you even belong in the church. What if you forget how to preach? What if you forget a parishioner's name? Look at everything you are responsible for when you lead a church. What if you forgot paperwork or how to do it? Are we supposed to just keep overlooking your memory issues forever because of your disability? Maybe our not ordaining you is a wake-up call that you don't belong in ministry and should look for another career somewhere else. By the way, there were several others from committees that had some comments about your interview; I can't remember who it was or what they said, but I do know I met with them this morning. But it doesn't matter that I can't remember what they said; what matters to us right now is we just don't know what to do with you because of your epilepsy and memory loss. So, we've made the decision we're not going to ordain you. Please feel free to try again next year. We actually hope you do. But so that you know, ordination for you is not going to happen this year. Who knows, maybe next year your epilepsy will be cured and we won't have anything to worry about. But like I've said, we just don't know what to do with you right now. Again, on behalf of the conference, I apologize. Well, I've got to go, I have another appointment I need to get to. You both take care and God Bless."

And that was the end of the meeting.

While it is true I didn't have any response to her discriminatory and narrow-minded comments, I did think to myself, *Leaders in a church conference are worried I might not remember a stranger's name whom I met a week ago at a funeral, yet here their representative sits and tells me she can't remember a colleague's name or something they said from that very morning.* How ironic, holding someone's disability against them but thinking nothing of using it to justify yourself and your decisions about another's capabilities.

In that moment, I knew I'd never truly belong in that conference. Sure, the higher ups could put on a good face, a face of acceptance, like the church usually does, but after that meeting I knew exactly how they truly felt about me. They didn't know what to do with me because I wasn't completely like them. I was different because I suffered from something that challenged them to look in broader ways to find the proper course of action needed in order for me to be accepted by them openly and lovingly, differences and all. But after that meeting, it was quite apparent the church didn't want anything to do with facing that challenge head on. That conversation in my former District Superintendent's office with a member from the church conference's Board of Ordained Ministry made it abundantly, albeit painfully clear, they were happy staying in their safe, narrow-minded tradition of "This is the way it's always been when we ordain someone."

That sentiment was backed up even more strongly a few years later when I once again tried for ordination. This time, the comment was made to me by another representative from that same conference's Board of Ordained Ministry: "When we ordain someone, we have to be sure we can appoint them anywhere within the boundaries of the conference. We can't keep making accommodations for those with disabilities."

If "they can't keep making accommodations for those with disabilities," what the hell will they do when the ordination candidate comes before their precious Board of Ordained Ministry in a wheelchair? What will they tell that disabled person? "Sorry, but not all of the churches and parsonages are handicapped accessible, and we can't afford to make them that way, so we don't have a place for you. But you understand, don't you?"

If the church "can't keep making accommodations for those with disabilities," but instead relies on flimsy excuses to justify that mindset, how is the world ever supposed to learn the better way? Isn't Christianity supposed to set the example of Christ's love and acceptance for all others to follow? As a minister, that's what I was taught in seminary and trained in conference workshops and what I tried to teach my parishioners. But after experiencing their uncalled-for discrimination firsthand, I knew otherwise. And the real hell of it is, the church is protected in their discrimination through the law of Ministerial Exception. I found that out the hard way as well. Because of the law of Separation of Church and State, the church can legally discriminate against its ministers all day long, 365 days of the year without threat of retribution; how nice for them. And yet, how just is that law?

Yet, I naively try to justify their discrimination to my wife; "I'm still with the conference, aren't I? They haven't told me they have no appointment for me."

"Yes, you're right, they haven't said that, at least not yet. But mark my words, the day is coming when it's going to happen. You know that as much as I do. We can both see the signs of it. Just look at your current church appointment, Nowheresville USA. And some appointment, let me tell you. When was the last time you had any kind of raise? They take you out of a large membership church where the possibility exists for you to go further in your career in ministry and put you here. And what about what you were told when you were offered this transfer, remember? If I'm not mistaken, I believe it was something along the lines of, 'If you don't take this appointment, because you're not ordained we're not sure if we'll have anything for you.' Real nice underhanded threat, let me tell you, 'Take it or you are out of here' was the basic message. And why were we moved in the first place? Oh, that's right, I remember now, because the senior pastor of the church where you were serving as an associate was an egocentric, self-centered, ass-kissing good ol' boy. I'm sure all of those conference higher-ups just love the way he sucks up to them," she says with sarcasm.

"You have no idea if he sucks up to anyone in the conference."

"Oh, come on! All anyone has to do is open their eyes to see it. And another thing, I still say he felt threatened by you. So, the simplest thing for him to do was tell his buddy, your beloved former District Superintendent Daniel, it's time for a change. And of course, him being one of the good ol' boys, the conference is going to side with him and move you, the guy with the disability that they don't know what to do with or can't keep making accommodations for."

"First of all, you know the conference rules of appointments. It's up to the bishop and cabinet who gets appointed where and when. We both know that's what I signed on for when I started serving this denomination. So please, let's not get into all of that now, there are more important things to think about, like getting you to the hospital to get that cut looked at." Good Lord, this is taking forever. "What's that?"

"What do you mean 'what's that?' Have you been ignoring me? Wouldn't be surprised if you were."

"No, I'm not ignoring you; that over there by the side of the road. What are those three kids doing?"

CHAPTER 10

"Help me, please. Please, someone help me. Stop it, it hurts so bad. Please don't hit me again. Please, oh please. What did I ever do to you guys? Please, stop...."

"Shut up and stop your whining, you faggot! Take your punishment like a man."

Punishment? Punishment for what, being who he is? Why is it so wrong for someone to be who they are? Why does someone have to hide who they are in order to be accepted by others? Because in reality, hiding one's true self isn't fully fitting in with others or being a part of their group. Rather, all hiding does is cover the truth so that others will accept you. And if that is the case, isn't that then more like an image and not the real person fitting in? And if it is just an image that is accepted, is that then saying people are more comfortable with images than with facts? But why is that? Could it be because images are easier to control and shape to fit one's preconceived ideas?

"Why do I deserve to be punished? What did I ever do to any of you guys? Please, stop."

"Look, faggot, I'm not telling you again, stop your whining and just shut up already. God, I can't stand to hear your prissy little voice. You make me sick, you know that? Nobody likes fags in this town or in this school, so guess what; you're the poster boy for any other faggot who thinks they can do what they want. They get one look at what we did to you and they'll know to keep their mouths shut and fag ways to themselves. See fellas, I told you this was going to be fun."

"Hey, what's that?"

"Those are car headlights. What the hell? Someone's pulling over."

"Come on guys, let's get out of here, someone's coming!"

"What do you think you're doing pulling over, my hand hurts, get me to the emergency room now, you idiot!" my wife shouts.

"But there's a kid laying over there. Someone's got to help him. I think those three boys that just drove off were beating him up," I reply.

"Oh sure, help some strange kid, but let me sit here in pain. That's real fair, let me tell you. I thought I was your wife? I thought you were supposed to put me and my needs above everyone else's, especially some stranger's. I really feel loved, let me tell you."

"Oh, knock it off. Someone has got to help that kid, look at him just lying there. What if that was you, wouldn't you want someone to stop and help you? We both know the answer to that question; remember the flat tire last year?"

Ignoring me, Ann continues her rant. "Like I said, run off and help some stranger and let me sit here bleeding like a stuck pig. Oh, just go and see if he needs help. I don't mind suffering at all. God, it's not like we're in the middle of nowhere; oh that's right, I forgot, we are," she says with definite sarcasm in her voice.

"Are you all right, son?" Again, a stupid question. Look at him bruised and bloodied; how could he be all right? "Come on, let's get you to your feet; can you stand?"

"I think so."

"Is there anywhere I can take you? Where are your folks? What were those other boys doing? Were they beating you up?" Whoa, enough of the questions already, you can see the kid is hurt and shaken up.

"Yes, they were beating me up, all you gotta do is open your eyes to see that," he says with sarcasm.

"Why were they beating you up? Did you provoke them in some way?"

"No, I didn't provoke them, they were beating on me because, um, I'm different," he continues with hesitation.

"Excuse me?"

"What, are you deaf or something? I said they were beating me up because I'm different."

"What makes you any different than they are?" I ask the boy, who looks like every other teenager I've ever seen.

"I'm not like them. I don't feel the same way they do, I don't like the things they like—hell, I don't even believe the way they believe—and because of that, I don't belong."

"What makes you so different? Besides, so what; who cares, none of us are the same as everyone else. That's what makes this world so incredible," I say. "Just because you're different doesn't mean you don't belong."

"Yeah right, maybe in your world, but not mine. Worse, it looks like they know my secret. But how did it get out? I've tried so hard to hide my secret and now the whole school probably knows it. My life is over. This is a nightmare. I knew I shouldn't have told Susan. But she would never rat me out. God, I shouldn't even be alive."

"You don't look different to me. Why don't you belong? What's making your life a nightmare and what's this secret you're trying so hard to hide?"

"You mean 'tried to hide.' And if I tell you, it won't be much of a secret, now would it?"

"But you said you told Susan, and from the looks of it the boys who beat you up know it too, so why can't I know?"

"Look, I'm just different, okay? Why don't you leave me alone? Nobody asked you to stop and help me. You know what, I'm fine without you. I don't need you to help me. I don't need anybody to help me. Just leave me alone. Who do you think you are anyway— God? Help this stranger, help that stranger. You know what, you don't know me and I don't know you, so why don't you just get outta my way and leave me alone? It will be better that way. I'm fine, just leave me alone already. Geez," he says to me with a definite hint of dismissiveness in his voice.

"Look kid, I'm sorry if you feel like I'm bothering you. And I know you've asked me at least five times now to leave you alone, but I'm not going to do that, and you want to know why: because you're hurt. And I'm not about to leave someone stranded at the side of the road in the middle of nowhere who I can clearly see is hurt. By the way, how did you get all the way out here? It's kind of deserted out here."

"The guys that beat me up asked me if I wanted to go for a ride with them. It felt so real when they asked. Like they wanted me to be a part of their group. They actually made me feel like I belonged. But then it all turned into a nightmare. They told me we were going to ride around town looking for girls, but then they brought me out here to the middle of fucking nowhere. God, the car ride was awful. The guy in the back seat made me do some really gross things to him and told me if I didn't he'd kill me. And the two in the front just laughed and kept urging him to torment me even more. It was horrible. I thought I was dead for sure."

"I'm so sorry it was horrible for you. But I am glad my wife and I came along when we did. By the way, no, I don't think I'm God. I am a minister though."

"Well, how nice for you. Guess what, Mr. Minister, not only was the car ride horrible for me, but my whole life has been pretty shitty and you can't change that; besides no one asked you to help, especially me, so get the hell out of here and for the last time, will you leave me alone already? Hell, it's because of your God that I'm ridiculed and looked down on," he says to me angrily.

"What do you mean it's because of God you're looked down upon? The God I serve is all-loving."

"Yeah right, sure He is. It's damn easy to say your God is all-loving, but what about the actions of the people who follow Him? Are their actions all-loving or are they judgmental and narrow-minded; 'Believe the way I believe, live the way I do or you're an unacceptable piece of shit?' Isn't that what you preach, Mr. Minister, this is against God's laws, that behavior is a terrible sin? It's like you stir up all these Bible beaters to hate and judge and then you hide their prejudice by making it seem like it is good religious living. You know what, here's an idea, why don't you go back to all of your 'loving' church folk and, like I said five or six times now, leave me the hell alone?"

"You can curse at me all you want, but I'm not going anywhere until I know you're all right, so you might as well get that through your head right now and stop fighting me. I'm not the enemy here, so stop making me one. Look, I have my wife in the car, I'm taking her to the emergency room because she got a bad cut on her hand and I think you should go with us and get checked out as well. Is there anyone I can call to tell them to meet us there, your parents or somebody else? By the way, I'm Pastor Todd. What's your name?"

"Why would you care about someone you don't even know? I thought strangers were supposed to ignore each other."

"Well kid, I look at it this way: if I don't care, who will? Besides, you don't know me either, or my story for that matter, now do you? You feel differently, said so yourself, right; guess what, kid, when I was your age I probably felt the exact same way. Still do," I mumble under my breath.

"What did you just say? Did you say something about me? You think I'm a weirdo don't you, that's what you just said to yourself, isn't it?"

"No, that's not what I said. And no, I don't want to get into this right now."

"Yeah right, I know what you're thinking, you can't fool me."

"Who ever said I was trying to fool you? Look, I stopped to help you because you looked like you were in trouble. What purpose would I have for trying to fool you or anyone else I don't know? Besides, how do you know what I'm thinking?"

Funny, here is someone else claiming they know what I'm thinking. Why do all of these people think they know my thoughts?

"Look, kid, I understand you are hurt and not thinking clearly, but you have no idea what I'm thinking. And you could say, 'Yeah right, all adults say they felt the same way when they were my age' but I'm telling you, with me it's the truth. And what I said under my breath is that my feelings of being discriminated against are still the truth today. Look, I have a phone on me. Here, use it to call your parents. Let them know what happened and then let me talk to them. Will you at least do that much? Come on, call your parents, please."

Immediately, a thought pops into the boy's head: how will his parents react when he calls them? What will he say to them? "Hi! Oh, by the way, I was just beaten up by three guys from school because they know I'm a homo." Yeah right, that will go over real big with them. Like the proverbial 'fart in church.' He can't call his parents. It would all be over. His secret would be out to the people who are supposed to love him unconditionally, and that will be the end of life as he knew it. At least his "normal" pretend life.

Gavin's mind goes back to September...

CHAPTER 11

"Time to get up and get ready for school," Gavin's mom called up the stairs.

Oh great, morning already? The summer flew by and now the first day of another stress-filled school year of inner turmoil and hiding the truth again. His mind was filled with the questions: what will the other kids say if they discover the secret he so carefully tries to hide? What will the teachers say? What will anyone say? "My stomach hurts," he muttered to himself.

Even though Gavin's known his truth since 4th grade, somehow it doesn't really matter. It never did. At his age, as with all kids, all that truly mattered was fitting in, making friends, and getting through another year of school unscathed—at least physically. Emotionally scathed—who cared about that? He'd been emotionally scarred for so many years already, so what harm could one more year do? Besides, emotions could be hidden but physical scars couldn't be, and everybody knows it's a lot easier to explain physical than emotional defects to someone. The truth was, emotions aren't as important as belonging is, right?

Anyone who's ever been a teenager knows life revolves around one thing, and only one thing: fitting in with the popular crowd. But considering all of the preconceived notions flying around the halls and classrooms, all of the generalizations that so easily fall from the mouths of others about "those kind of people," or considering the fact that with increased age there seems to come narrower and narrower mindsets, (hell, all he had to do was look at the adults around him to see that), if his secret ever did come out, he knew fitting in would never be an option. Instead, he'd be black-balled and banished to the realms of some unseen and unimaginable hell. As such, he made the decision a long time ago that the other kids finding out his secret would never happen. He made the decision he would always keep it hidden, no matter how many emotional scars it would inflict upon him. And he'd do whatever it took to make sure he kept it concealed. But even he had to admit the inner pain this secret caused could be unbearable some days and make appearing "normal" in public seemingly impossible.

After all, it's so much easier being yourself when you are by yourself anyway. There is no one around to judge you or think you're weird or whatever it is other people think. Think about it: when you are by yourself, you can let it all "hang out," so to speak. As an example, even if you're not very good at it, you can sing or dance or do whatever it is that makes you feel good and whole.

Yet thinking more about it, what good is it to be yourself in front of yourself? After all, you already know who you are, don't you? You know the truth that lives inside of you and ultimately defines who you are, what makes you happy and feel more complete. So, while it may be easier staying there, does being by yourself lead to wholeness of life and living?

Further, whether we realize it or not, a direct result of knowing our inner truth is that you or I or any one of us already have the capacity to accept ourselves for who we are. Unfortunately, while we may be terrified the world won't accept our truth and just dismiss us as weird and cast us aside like a piece of garbage, how often do we dismiss our true selves and not only tell, but actually convince ourselves, we are truly as worthless as society determines those like us to be?

Yet, while it may not seem like it at the time, in the end it definitely is worth taking the risk of stepping into the unknown and showing our true selves to others, because those very truths are what define us and make us whole. Further, while it may seem terrifying, there actually is an incredible feeling of freedom that comes when we step out from behind any and all societal or self-imposed curtains of hiding.

Another fact we must take into consideration is, as long as we hide our true selves from the rest of the world, how will they ever learn to fully accept us and have the opportunity to love us for who we truly are? They won't. It just can't happen. But then again if it doesn't happen, if others don't accept us for who we really are, so what, who cares? It sure is safer to hide the truth and stay locked inside a bubble of self-defined security anyway, isn't it? Nobody can deny that, can they?

Look at the life Gavin has built for himself in his mind. While he is just starting high school, in his mind he is already 'lord' of the school. All the other kids adore him. He is the one they follow. He is the one who holds all the power and whatever he says or does is what the other kids will say or do. They all follow his lead completely. In his mind, his fictitious life is incredible.

His real life on the other hand...that's a different story. In reality, Gavin's life is filled with doubt and fear. His is a life filled with self-denial and feelings of worthlessness. So, for Gavin, while real life is nothing but a bunch of shit, fantasy life is something to cherish and hold on to.

"There is no doubt about it, no one can ever find out about my secret; no one. I'll do whatever I have to, to make sure they don't," Gavin said to himself.

"Did you hear me? It's time to get up; we have a lot to do this morning, it being your first day of high school and all! Let's go!"

"I'll be there in a minute, Mom!" he called downstairs. God, why couldn't she understand? Why couldn't anyone understand how hard all of this was? Especially the first day in high school. But then Gavin suddenly came to a realization that caused him to pause and ask himself, how could his mother understand something she didn't know about?

Elementary school is one thing. Kids are just that, kids. And little kids accept everyone because they seemingly don't know any better. Sure, middle school is a little harder, but the truth is that kids are still accepting because they are still young. But high school is a different environment altogether. Now kids are growing up, becoming teenagers and young adults. Now they are trying to find their place, jockeying for status, being the 'top dog' in high school, so they'll do anything they can to get to and keep that position. Everything from throwing insults without regard to who gets hurt, playing mental games that devalue and cause doubt, to straight out physical abuse. All in the hope of getting to some lofty position of acceptance and being a part of the 'cool crowd.'

What if the truth about him did come out now that he was starting high school? How would he ever survive the narrow-mindedness and all of the preconceived notions about what 'those kind of people' are all about, what they believe, how they act? Can't think about that now; too many other things to worry about. Besides, how could anyone understand if they didn't know him and instead merely judged him according to their preconceptions?

This was going to be so hard. "Just let me lay here for five more minutes, give myself a little more time to build the facade I know I will have to present every day in order to survive, to be all right. I can do this, I know I can do this. But God, this is so hard…" Gavin said to himself.

"What would you like for breakfast? We have the cereal you like, there's frozen waffles, or toast. What would you like? Sorry, but we're running late so we don't have time for eggs," his mother called up the stairs.

"Anything for breakfast is fine with me," he called back. Eating breakfast was one thing, but the realities of life, and swallowing those truths, now those were something else entirely.

Actually, what he wanted was to be a different person than who he currently was; that was what he would like more than anything. He'd like to be someone who no longer had to hide, but was fully accepted and not looked at like some kind of freak no matter his beliefs or lifestyle. But then again, if he wanted to be different, why didnt he just do it already? Why was he choosing to live in obscurity? That's what everyone where he lived thought anyway; his lifestyle was a choice, nothing more, nothing less. Hell, if that was true and this "gay thing" was nothing more than a choice, why wasn't it easier, why did it take a hold of you and not let go? 'Cause it sure wasn't letting go of him.

And while in some ways things do seem to be getting a bit better in the world today, he somehow knew that it was not totally possible for complete change and acceptance to occur then. Probably not even the next five years. But maybe one day the world would be different; that would be nice. Maybe one day he can be who he truly is, and the world will be all right with that and accept him and then he'll belong. "Yeah right, like that's going to happen; today is today and I have to live with that," he said to himself with forced strength because this inner argument was exhausting him.

Maybe one day. But for right now, in this moment of his life, the bright spot that showed through the darkness of this whole mess was he knew he had one friend who would stick by him to the very end. At least, that's what she told him. Yet even though she may have said, "We'll always be friends, no matter what..." and he may have believed her, were those words truly from her heart, or merely from her mouth?

Because then the thought came to him: sticking by him because he is quiet or shy is one thing, but what if Susan found out about the real him and why he was so introverted? What would happen then; would she stick by him when those chips are down? He'd like to think the answer was 'yes' and yet he couldn't help but ask himself would he remain loyal if the roles were reversed and Susan was the one who revealed such a major secret to him? Again, isn't high school all about belonging, being seen with the right crowd? If he stuck by someone so different, would anyone want anything to do with him? No, probably not, because in order to be accepted and fit in with the "right" crowd, there's no way he would truly stick by the 'freak.' So why should anyone stick by him, the queer, if the ultimate truth came out? After all, isn't fitting in just as important to everyone else as it is to him? That's a no brainer; of course, it is.

And fitting in—or actually, not fitting in—is another reason to tell Susan. For you see, Susan wasn't accepted by the other kids. At one time she was, but now things were vastly different. To put it bluntly, Susan's overweight. Or as the other kids, and even adults, say, "She's fat." And because of that, Susan was seen as an embarrassment to the "cool" kids. And because all of the others want to be seen as one of the "cool kids," she was now considered an embarrassment by all of them. No one wanted to be her friend, no one wanted to be seen hanging around with her, she was no longer looked upon as being worthy of their time or attention, but was instead ridiculed, reviled, and rejected. Gavin had heard it said so often, "There is no hope for her, who would ever love someone so fat, what's wrong with her, her parents should sew her mouth shut so she stops eating." Pain-filled comments that, if she would ever hear them, would hurt Susan in ways Gavin could only imagine. And because of all of those heartless and thoughtless comments, he didn't even want to think about what the others would say about him if they knew his secret.

Gavin would never forget the day Susan came to him crying. It was another boring, ordinary day in school. A day where the cool kids acted like they were the end all to end all. In their minds surely everyone else was comparing themselves to them. The clothes they wore, the things they said. Even the ways they rolled their eyes if they found something stupid or weird. Surely all of the other kids wanted to be just like them. Then, completely opposite of the "cool" kids were the "nerdy" kids. The kids that no one wanted to associate with because they were just too strange or geeky or "out there." And in between both groups were all of the other faceless, nameless kids who were just there. The kids that were neither cool nor geeky. The place where Gavin and Susan found themselves "living."

But just as it is true in the world at large, the reality is even in school there is a large cross section of people with lives and secrets and joys and sorrows. The reality is there are kids from single parent homes, kids who are adopted, kids who have brothers and sisters and kids who are only children. So many different personalities and beliefs all in the same place for the exact same reason, to learn, to grow, and to hopefully come to some understanding that even though everyone is different, everyone has value and is in so many ways important. And while all the kids in Gavin's school were different, somehow it all seemed to work. At least on some surface level it did.

That was, until events occurred like the one that did that day several years ago. Stuck in one of her school books, Susan found the letter from her supposed friends. "We don't want to be your friend anymore. You're fat and ugly and all of the other kids think the same," it cruelly proclaimed without the least hesitation. And it was in that moment Susan felt unwanted, isolated, and unloved. What had been seen as ordinary just a few moments before took on a completely different meaning. Now instead of being a part of "the crowd," Susan felt like this "thing" that had no place in school, let alone society. Susan began to believe she didn't belong and her supposed circle of confidants made that abundantly and painfully clear that dreadful day.

And even though Gavin could do his best to hide his gayness and protect himself from the meanness of the other kids, there was no way Susan could hide her weight. It was out there for the whole world to see. She was like some oversized target the enemy could just so easily take cheap shots at until they found their mark. Problem was, the enemies that were shooting at Susan were other human beings. But why was it okay for human beings to lash out against and devalue other human beings?

As a result, the bond between Gavin and Susan was sealed. The faggot and the fatty, two lonely, wounded souls reaching out to each other looking for at least some small semblance of hope and acceptance. How pathetic was that, right? Why does society have to be so damn judgmental?

CHAPTER 12

On top of that, Gavin also had to consider how he was being raised and the mindset of his parents. He had to look at how his parents were and take into consideration how the town he lived in and the church he belonged to still were, even now in the 21st century.

God, it was hard living in that kind of town. Sure, adults think it's quaint and all, but for a kid, especially a teenager, it was boring. It felt so suffocating. Small town living might be right for some people, but not for him. Talk about a town with no red light. Not only weren't there any red lights, there weren't any businesses either. Actually, in his opinion, the only things that did exist in that town were anger and depression and reminiscing about the "good old days" when the town was...

As a matter of fact, there wasn't much more there other than dilapidated old houses in desperate need of repair and frustrated people whose main goals in life seemed to be to keep everyone else down. If someone from that town did happen to find some small measure of success and lived in a nicer house or made a little more money, the other people would say they were happy for the person, but were they really? Especially when the gossip started and the negative remarks ruled the day...

"Who did he sleep with to make it?"

"Whose ass did she kiss to get such a cushy job?"

"So what if she has a good job, she should be home with her kids where she belongs."

"Sure, they might have a nice house, but I wouldn't want the taxes on it and look who their neighbors are..."

And then on top of the gossip there was the fact that to most of the people living there, church was everything and if you didn't feel and believe the same way the other Christians did, personal feelings didn't matter. He saw that at least a thousand times. Going against the church was going against God. And you don't go against God no matter what. You suck it up instead, pray for forgiveness, healing or release, and wait for God to cleanse you of this terrible sin or disease or whatever it is you want to call it. But what good is praying if the words aren't followed up by some positive action? It's like, "Turn our problems over to God in prayer and He'll take care of them and if He doesn't, oh well that's His will." And you know what they say, "Thy kingdom come, thy will be done..." The thing Gavin couldn't understand was, why is it God's will to reward liars and cheats but people who try to live good clean lives are given the shaft?

All of these thoughts raced through his mind, causing him to panic even more. What if his parents did find out? What would they do? They would kill him, that's what they'd do; no, maybe not physically, but mentally for sure. There was no doubt in his mind about that whatsoever. They'd look at him like he was some kind of a freak that didn't deserve their love and understanding. He could see them ignoring him, turning their backs on him, disowning him, and then what would he do? He knew if his secret ever came out, it would totally destroy the image of their wholesome American family. The neighbors would talk. New fodder for gossip. "Destroy whoever isn't like us." He could hear it all.

And then that voice inside his head spoke out loudly and clearly once again: "What the hell are you thinking, telling someone? You gotta bury your secret even further, you idiot."

"Shake a leg up there kid, we're running out of time," his mother called up the stairs for the fourth time.

It would destroy his mother, he was convinced of that. She would never be able to survive a scandal like that. And it would be a scandal. He was certain his parents would never accept him. From their previous behavior and statements, he could pretty much guarantee their response would at the very least be "Send him away. Get him fixed…" Like he was broken or something. He wasn't broken, he was just different. Why was it so wrong to be different anyway? Why couldn't people accept you for who you were? Why must people be so damn judgmental? Did it make them feel better about themselves? Did it give them some kind of power that they wouldn't have otherwise? Why were their narrow-minded opinions so right and others, who maybe think a little more broadly, so wrong? He didn't understand. Actually, he wasn't sure he wanted to understand in the first place.

But then it occurred to him, by not opening himself up to at least trying to understand others, by just shutting himself off from what surely was a reality that lived not only in his life but in the lives of so many others, by not definitively sticking by another no matter who or what they were, was he allowing himself to become just like those who were narrow-minded and conventional? The truth of the matter was yes, he was. Because the reality was if he allowed himself to believe that, then he wasn't accepting of others for who they were, just as he feared they wouldn't be accepting of him for who he was. And what good did that do? Wouldn't it help the world to be more accepting of others, whether known or a stranger, and not just casually give people excuses to continue to disregard others because they are different?

Ed. D'Agostino

Further, he was not only allowing others' opinions and beliefs to have ultimate power and dominion over his life, but by hanging onto a narrow unaccepting mindset, wasn't he also allowing his personal opinions to have power over other people's lives and dictate what they should believe, or the way they should act or live, in order to ultimately be accepted by him? And as a result, if they didn't fit in with his opinions or didn't measure up to the standards he had established for them in his mind, then just like they didn't want to have anything to do with him, he wouldn't want to have anything to do with them? And by not wanting to have anything to do with each other because of misconception and opinion, how was that good? How was that helpful for growth and understanding? It wasn't and it never would be because, for example, by allowing the value of his life to be determined by others, the reality was it wasn't his life—his life was being dictated by those whom he was trying so vehemently to fit in with, the same people he was trying to hide his true self from. And so it is with all others, not just ourselves.

As a result, Gavin realized he wasn't truly living his life; rather, he was living an image of a life. The question was, by living an image of a life that fit into society's standards, would his pretend life ever be truly happy and fulfilling for him? In other words, was it a true life, or was it a pretend conventional life just so he could say he belonged and no one would talk about or disregard him?

Conventional. God, how he hated that word. It was so stifling, so restrictive. If something wasn't conventional, it was just too weird, too out there to be taken with any real seriousness, wasn't it? Was that him, too weird, too out there to be taken seriously? Did that, in and of itself, make him want to hide the truth even more because the fear of losing something as important as acceptance weighed more heavily upon him than the importance of any truth? Good lord, he was just a kid, why did he have to go through all of this bullshit? Besides, what did kids know about real truth anyway?

One thing Gavin finally came to see as truth was that his best friend Susan would always be there for him. After much anguish and inner turmoil, he made a life-altering decision to tell his secret to her, a secret most would see as unforgivable. But, as amazing as it may seem, after telling her his "unforgivable" secret, her response was the exact opposite of not showing him acceptance. Instead, Gavin felt she truly listened to him. She heard his words, she felt his fear, and more importantly, she never judged him. She actually hugged him and told him it would be all right, she would always be there for him. That day would change him forever. But the night before almost convinced him to remain hidden in a cycle of fear and doubt.

CHAPTER 13

The night before the day Gavin decided to share his secret with Susan was perfect in so many ways. The sky was dark and full of stars, there was a light breeze blowing, and the temperature was perfect for sleeping with the windows open. There was, however, one thing that wasn't perfect. He just could not fall asleep. His mind was too consumed with thoughts about what would happen the next day. And while he tried to convince himself that tomorrow would be the day that he was going to at least confide in one person, and that person was going to be his friend Susan, he was still filled with doubt and fear about his decision. Instead of enjoying the feeling of release one gets when they fall into deep sleep, he, on the other hand, was consumed by worry and dread. It gnawed at his mind like some ravenous vulture gnawing on a carcass and no matter how much he tried not to think about it, it invaded his thoughts.

As the night got darker, his mind was continually consumed with the question, "Should I tell her?" Maybe he should keep it a secret and let things be the way they had always been; wouldn't that be best for all involved? After all, why make waves? Why rock the boat, so to speak? Keeping his secret would definitely be the easiest and safest thing to do. And yet, keeping his secret would be like selling himself out, wouldn't it? Keeping his secret would give him the excuse to continue being untrue to himself. And what did anyone ever get from untruth, especially to themselves? But who cared? What the hell was the big deal about being true to yourself? Why is that so damn important anyway? How far did that ever get anyone? How far would it get him?

What if after telling Susan, her response wasn't in the accepting way he had imagined? What if his best friend turned her back on him? What if she tossed him aside like some worthless good-for-nothing faggot? What if he lost his best friend because of it? Again, what if, what if, what if. All of the 'what ifs' filled his mind that night with doubt and despair and took away any confidence he may have built up the moment when he first decided to confide in her. What if this or that was her reaction; then what? What would he do? He would have confided in someone who would take his secret and blab it to everyone else to try to gain some semblance of footing she had lost with the other kids. What if she did that? Where would that leave him? Never belonging, that's where. On the outside, alone, looking in, desperately trying to find his place among his classmates. He could imagine just how awful that would be. Maybe it would be best if he didn't tell her. Yeah, in the long run that would be best, wouldn't it? Or would it?

The night seemed endless. Hour upon hour of torment, doubt, and worry. Should he tell her? Maybe he shouldn't. What would happen if he did? What would happen if he didn't and she found out another way? If she did find out from someone else, at least he could lie and tell her it was not true. How could she prove it anyway, especially if it didn't come from him directly? Wouldn't it be better to keep living the lie? What if she turned her back on him? What if she wasn't as open-minded and accepting as he thought? The torture, the anguish, the doubt, and despair. It just didn't seem worth it.

But if he didn't tell her, then he'd have to keep living a lie, and not only with his best friend but with everyone else, including himself, and how comforting would that be? Is living a lie ever worth it? Does sacrificing who you truly are just to be what others want you to be give anyone a true feeling of success and acceptance, or does it leave this hole of doubt and confusion?

His grandfather used to say to him, "It's always darkest just before the dawn." What if it wasn't? What if he told her, and his life got even darker? What if...? What if...? What if...?

After what was a truly exhausting and seemingly endless night, like it always does, dawn arrived. Funny, no matter how dark the night seems to get there is no stopping the sun from rising. A new day always comes filled with new possibilities, new life, new opportunities, new everything just waiting for every one of us to embrace the newness it holds. That is, of course, unless we choose instead to only hold on to the darkness of the night before.

And then something other than the sun dawned on him; maybe that was what his grandpa meant with his corny saying. Sure, things may look dark and overwhelming now, but a new day will always come. The thing we have to understand is, the ways in which we embrace and live this new day ultimately determine how bright and hope-filled it will be or how dark and hopeless it will stay. The choices are ours to make every single day, and what we choose determines how our day will go.

With that in mind, as he got out of bed that morning, he told himself, "I've made my decision, and I intend to stick to it. No more hiding, no more allowing fear to control my life and destiny. No more pretending. Pretending, hiding, fear are nothing more than bullshit excuses to not try. Today will be a day for real change and growth, no matter how small that change or growth may be. And I've decided it's going to be a good day no matter the outcome."

"What are you up to today, kid?"

"I figured I'd ride over to Susan's house and see if she wanted to hang out together." As soon as he heard himself say the words, the doubts once again flooded in upon his mind and so he added, "But now I'm not sure what I'm going to do."

"Isn't she home?"

"Yeah, she's home, I'm just not sure I want to hang out with her today." *Wait a minute, I made a decision and I'm sticking to it. Of course I'm going to go see Susan. And when I tell her my secret, I know she will love and accept me for who I am and it will be all right*, he reassured himself.

But unfortunately, on his way to Susan's house, his mind was once again filled with uncertainties and doubts. Filled with what if... what if...what if...Riding his bike, with all of those 'what ifs' floating around in his head, was probably the hardest thing he had ever done in his life. At least that's how it felt in that moment. But no matter how many 'what ifs' tried to get in the way of this journey, something inside of him kept motivating him to keep peddling. It was as though there was another voice inside of him that kept telling him, "Keep moving forward. You can do this. All of those doubts you are having are nothing more than mind games. Embrace the fear that lives inside of you. Respect it. But don't let it determine the course you take on this journey to wholeness and truth."

As he rode, he tried desperately not to think so much about the decision he had made. Instead, he tried to convince himself to look at the trees, look at the birds. "I wonder if it's going to rain. I wonder when it will get cooler? I wonder when...?"

He thought about how long the summer seemed to drag on, and yet it was over so quickly. He thought about the family vacation to the beach this year and how his little brother loved jumping in the waves. He thought about anything else but what he was about to do.

But the closer he got to Susan's house, the more he realized that no matter how much he forced himself to think about so many other things, the truth of what he was about to do was still there. Because who he is was always going to be there, and pretending it wasn't would never change that truth in any way. Yes, he may mask it or hide it. But change it? Never.

CHAPTER 14

"Hey, Gavin, where you goin'?"

"Hey, Kevin! How you doin'? I'm going over to Susan's house to see if she wants to ride bikes or whatever. What are you up to?"

"You want to be seen with that fatso? Are you crazy man? You hear what the other kids say about her. You should come with me instead, I'm meeting up with a bunch of other guys for a game of ball."

"But I already told Susan I was on my way over."

"So what, let her fat ass swing in the breeze. Come on, let's go hook up with the other guys."

Invited to play ball with the other fellas? Hmm, it appeared he hid his secret well. Maybe he should just keep his mouth shut after all and forget about what was beginning to look more and more like a crazy decision to tell Susan.

Once again, the question "How will she react when I tell her?" rushed into his mind. The reality was he had no way of knowing for sure. What if she didn't want to have anything to do with him anymore? What if she did blab it to the other kids? What if she used it against him in some way to hurt him, make him suffer? After all, she lived in this town too. What if...what if... what if...?

"You know what, Kevin, I think I will join you if you need an extra player."

"We can always use extra players, you know that. Come on, let's go."

Riding to the park was a lot easier than riding to Susan's house, that's for sure. Was that because he was riding toward something that was fun and where he felt like he was accepted and away from something that could have been full of doubt and possible rejection?

When they got to the park, the other boys were already there waiting for Kevin.

"Hey, guys, look who I found on the way here, Gavin! I invited him to play ball with us. Come on, let's choose up sides and get this game going.'"

Although she lived only twenty minutes from his house, because of this change in plans it took Gavin over two hours to get to Susan's. Not so ironically, when he did finally reach her house, the same terror he had so desperately tried to avoid and that actually disappeared in the fun of playing ball hit once again like a storm of uncertainty. How would she react? Would she throw him out and never speak to him again? Would he lose his best friend forever? God, this was so hard. While he thought the bike ride to her house was the hardest journey he had ever been on, he suddenly discovered that walking to her front door was ten times harder.

"Hello, Mrs. Williams. Is Susan home?"

"Just a minute dear, I'll get her. Suzy, dear, that nice young boy Gavin is here to see you!"

"Just a minute, Mom. Be right down," Susan called from upstairs.

As opposed to Susan's house, which was the perfect size, his house was a big old barn of a place. And unlike Susan's parents, who were very laid back, his parents were very conservative. They were frequently in church, every Sunday for sure, as well as many times during the week for Bible study or other stuff. His dad was an accountant and his mom stayed home to take care of him and his younger brother, which was how the people who lived here thought it should be. The woman stays home and takes care of the family and the father makes the money. None of this "women are equal to men" crap. There's no place in real society for that stupidity. And whereas Susan's dad drove a sporty sedan, his dad drove a minivan and every year his family went to the beach for vacation. Although on the outside it would appear to everyone else they had it all, a nice house, a loving family, vacations, the works, there was a secret that loomed over his family that even they didn't know about. A secret his best friend Susan would find out about today. He was about to reveal to her that he was one of "those kind of people."

And what does one of those kinds of people look like? To most of humanity, especially those from Napier Springs, they are the kind of person that has no place in a wholesome society, God's country. They are the kind of person who is seen as an abomination in the eyes of God and in the eyes of true men and women of God. God-fearing men and women know the truth and anything other than that truth is irrelevant, false, and worthless and the only thing any kind of false verity will do is lead one astray. All it will do is tempt others to live in sinful ways, chasing after some preconceived notion of what an easy devotion is or looks like. There are no values in easy truth.

"Won't you come in, dear? Susan will be right down. Would you like a glass of milk or a home baked cookie?" Susan's mother asked him.

"Sure, sounds great." Susan's mom made the best cookies he had ever tasted.

After Susan's mom left the living room, he started to look around. He always found himself to be fascinated by all of the old stuff they had sitting around. Some of it had to be hundreds of years old, or at least that was what he thought.

"Here we are, dear, a nice glass of fresh milk and some home-made cookies. What were you looking at?"

"What is that?" asked Gavin. "It looks like an old telescope."

"It is an old telescope. It belonged to my grandmother. She inherited it from her mother, my great-grandmother. My grandmother told me that her father, my great-grandfather, gave it to my great-grandmother on their wedding day. I still have the note he had with it when he gave it to her. He told her to use it to look at the stars and tell him which one she wanted and he would spend his life trying to pick it out of the sky just for her. So romantic. My grandmother used to tell me stories about my great-grandparents when they were first married and came to this country. They were sure no one would accept them because he was from England and she was from Africa. They weren't your typical couple. They were different."

"How were they different?" Gavin asked.

"She was black and he was white, and to most people at that time different races marrying was an unforgivable sin. But to my great-grandparents, it was no big deal. They were who they were; they were in love with each other and that was the most important thing."

She continued, "Actually, that is the most important thing for any one of us to remember, and probably the most important lesson I ever learned from all those stories about my great-grandparents; never be afraid to be who you truly are. If others don't accept you for who you truly are, how important are they in the first place? Probably not very. Lord, they must have had some tough times, the way others would treat them. They were treated like they had some kind of disease or something. Even their little ones suffered from the cruelty of it all, including my grandmother. But I'm sure you don't want to hear about my family's history, you came to see Susan."

"Your grandfather was from England and your grandmother was from Africa?"

"No, my grandparents were from this country. It was my great-grandfather, not my grandfather, who was originally from England. My great-great grandparents and my great-grandfather came to this country when he was a young man."

"So, your great-grandfather was white and your great-grandmother was black and they were married?"

"Yes, they were married."

"But I thought that was illegal."

"It was illegal. Actually, their marriage was never recognized by anyone else. They didn't have a marriage license or anything. But that didn't matter to my great-grandparents. They loved each other, and no one was going to tell them to feel any differently. It was their love for each other that got them through what were some of the most difficult times of their lives. I can't imagine what they were put through; it must have been horrible."

"How did they meet?" Gavin asked.

"My great-grandfather was a minister and he was on a missionary trip to Africa. Actually, when he got back from that trip with my great-grandmother and told the church he had married this black girl, they told him he wasn't fit to be a minister because he had married a black woman and they threw him out of the church. Apparently, he was so crushed by it he never went back into ministry ever again, even after having served the church for many years. It was so sad. But enough about that, like I said you didn't come here to listen to a bunch of old stories that wouldn't interest you any way..."

CHAPTER 15

John Wilson met Adannaya (or as she was known in America: Anna) on his first missionary trip to Western Africa. And even though they were from different worlds and had different beliefs, John instantly knew there was something about this girl. He felt an immediate attraction to her. But was this feeling of attraction real, or was it just some form of insanity brought about by being in a new and unknown place? After all, everything here was different and exciting compared to the mundane routines of his life in the States. Besides, look at her, she's black and he's white, she's a "savage" and he's, by degrees, refined. People, at least his people, would never accept it—accept her—and yet there was something about her.

Trying to put the feeling out of his mind, John concentrated on the project at hand: digging a well for Adannaya's village. It seemed that fresh water was a precious commodity in that part of Africa and a well would definitely help bring deeper hope to what appeared to his outsider's view to be a very hopeless existence. Again, look at his life; he had easy access to plenty of fresh water, plenty of food, clean clothes, a nice house. The list seemed endless. In comparison, Adannaya and her family had nothing, or at least not much. Along with her parents, grandmother, and three sisters, she lived in a shack that was no bigger than John's living room, there wasn't much to eat, her clothes were dirty and worn, no water, hot dry conditions, dirt everywhere; yet, Adannaya was happy. She was happy! Her entire family was. But how? How could she or anyone who lived in that place possibly be so happy in those circumstances? They constantly had smiles on their faces. And they weren't just pasted-on fake smiles. No, theirs was a real down to the bones light-up-their-entire-face smile. But look at this place, look at their lives; what lived inside of these people that gave them such joy? John was about to find out.

That evening, when it was time for John and the other people on his missionary team to sit down and share a meal with the villagers, John's eyes were opened to something more real and life-affirming than he had ever thought possible. Not only did the people of this native girl's village give thanks to their God for the meager meal placed before them, they served their guests first and gave them the best and biggest portions of the meal. Here they were, strangers to each other, but that didn't matter. All that mattered to these humble villagers was that all of them, including the strangers, were together. And some would say they gave their guests the biggest and best portions of the meal because they were there to dig a well for them, but to John there was more to it than that.

"Hello, my name is Adannaya. What is your name? I heard the others calling you John. Is this right?"

"Yes, my name is John."

"It is so nice to meet you, John. And thank you for helping my village have water. We are very thankful you have come. We have been praying to God to send someone and here you are. We did not know what we were going to do. So many of the people in my village are old and the walk to the well to get water two times a day is getting very hard. So many women become sick or hurt trying to carry the heavy water so far. It is a terrible thing. This well that you and the others are digging will be a true blessing to my people."

"I am very grateful we could be here to help you and your people."

"I just hope you don't look down on us like we are foolish or stupid. You are so worldly and we are so simple. My village, my home, must look like a mess to someone like you and the other people with you."

"Not at all. I am puzzled by something though."

"What does puzzled mean?"

"It means I'm confused or don't understand something. Does that make sense to you?"

"Yes. But what is, as you say, puzzling you?" Adannaya asked.

"I just can't understand how you and the people of your village are so happy when you are surrounded by what looks like so much misery. How is that possible? I know I would be very angry and upset."

"It only looks like misery to you because you are only seeing what is on the outside. When you look at the whole picture, then you will come to know why we are so happy. What you see as so little is quite a lot to us. Ever since I was a little girl, I was told that who is around you, not just what is around you, is what is most important. Me and my people are so happy because we are around people who love us and treat us like we matter. Like you and your people treat us. You all traveled very, very far to help people you never met have fresh water. Why would you do that if we didn't matter, even if it is just a little bit? When my sisters or I were younger and we would complain about how poor we were and not having a nice house or other things, my father would sit us down and tell us to really look around us and tell him what we saw. His lesson to us was that it is not what the house you live in looks like, but who lives in that house with you that matters. And that taught us to look more deeply and with bigger hearts. Do you see what I mean? It's very sad when the only thing people see is what is on the outside. Doesn't what is on the inside of a person have value too?"

He knew she was right, but he didn't know how to answer her. For being an uneducated girl from some obscure African village, she was more intelligent and insightful than he was because she not only looked with her eyes but, more importantly, she saw with her heart. And what her heart showed her was the world. At that moment he didn't feel very worldly or refined. Instead he felt extremely selfish, stupid, and small.

As the village chief stood to speak, many of the others sat down. Those that remained standing because they were cooking or serving the meal immediately stopped what they were doing and bowed their heads in respect. "It is an honor to welcome our distinguished guests. I want to thank them for their hard work making our village better. The well they are digging will bring fresh water to our village, which brings us fresh hope."

The rest of the villagers cried out, "Useko! Useko! Useko!" Useko means "Thank you" in Adannaya's village language of Fulfulde, and saying it three times showed much gratitude.

That first night filled with welcome and gratitude from strangers halfway around the world was just the beginning of the transformation John's life was about to undergo.

"I must say, your grasp of the English language is quite good," John said to Adannaya.

"Thank you. We have discovered that in order to live in this world, we must learn your English. Actually, the teacher that I had when I went to the village school was also a missionary from your country. And while he encouraged us to speak our native language at home, in school we had to speak in English. It is still the same today. The village children must speak English in school, but at home may speak Fulfulde."

"But isn't that hard for you? I know it would be hard for me."

"Not really. Did you know there many different ways to speak just in this part of my country?"

"That must be very confusing for you."

"It is, but it would be more confusing if I did not respect the person who speaks differently. If I think to myself, 'My way of talking is the right way and they are wrong in how they say things,' I won't learn their language. And if I don't learn their language, how can I speak to them? I can't. So, if I don't try to speak like they speak, there is no hope of communication and I will turn my back on them. But I have learned to talk like they talk and they have learned to talk like I talk so we can live together in harmony and respect. It is a very beautiful thing."

"But what if you don't like or understand the way they talk?"

"Just because I don't like the way someone talks or fully understand them doesn't mean I can't accept them, does it? I mean, if we just go around not accepting people who talk differently or that we don't completely understand, where will we end up? Take me, for instance; I do not talk like you do. I do not dress like you. I am a stranger to you. But just because I am different from you in so many ways, does that give you the right not to accept me because I am who I am?"

"I guess living in joy and harmony is a beautiful thing, but so is this place. I've never seen so many stars in my life and the landscape is breathtaking," John said.

"Yes, every night I look up in the sky at all of the beautiful stars and wish I could reach up and grab one and put it in my pocket to remind me that even in the darkness there are still many beautiful lights. That must sound silly to you."

"Not at all. Actually, I think it is a beautiful wish, one that every one of us should have."

"How many stars do you think are up there?" Adannaya asked John.

"I have no idea, but I do know they sure are lovely."

"So many of my people and people from other tribes look up at them and use them to help find their way. No matter where they are at night, they can always tell which direction they have to go to get home just by looking at the stars. I think that is amazing, as you say in your language."

"Sea captains and other explorers do the very same thing," John replied. "They believe that by looking to the light they will always find their way in the darkness. And yet we seem so lost in the light. How is that possible?"

"Because when we are in the light we think we don't have to really look," Adannaya replied. "I think it is like what you said to me about guessing living in joy and harmony is beautiful. Why do you only guess that, don't you know for sure?" Adannaya asked.

"No, I don't."

"Why not? Your life must be magical," Adannaya said. "I'm sure you have a life I can only dream about, a house that is beautiful, so many things, lovely clothes. All the people in your country must be so happy having so much. What more could you want? It is like a dream to me. Having all of those things, how could you want anything else? I would not."

"Yes, I do have many things, but you have shown me the one thing I don't have, something that I want more than anything."

"What could this be, this thing that you want so badly?"

"I want your joy, Adannaya. And I want your light. Like the night sky is lit up with stars, there is a light that shines from you that is wonderful."

"I do not understand. You must have a lot of joy in your life."

"In ways yes, I do, but it is nothing compared to what I see in you and your people, because my joy depends upon having things around me. I'm sure you all were joyful before we even got here, weren't you?"

"Yes, we were."

"But how could that be? What I mean by that is, I see how you and your people are living in very difficult times without water close by, and yet you are still happy. Actually, after the well has been dug and my team and I are gone, you and the people of your village will still be living in hard times. But that doesn't seem to dampen your spirits at all. How is that possible?"

"'Dampen?' What does this word 'dampen' mean?"

"Dampen means to make it feel like less," John replied.

"No, our joy will not be less, John, because we will not only have our own well, but we will still have each other. Plus, this well will help people from other villages."

"How will it help other villages?" John asked.

"People from my village will get word to other villages that we have a well here and they are welcomed to come here and get fresh water anytime they like. I'm sure it will bring many new faces to our little village, which means we will be able to make more friends of people we have never met," Adannaya said.

Was Adannaya saying having each other is the key to finding happiness? But what if the other person is 'revolting' or unacceptable in some way? What if they are a stranger? Or must we look at them in a different way? Instead of only seeing them as strangers, must we begin to see others as fellow human beings we just don't know yet?

The six weeks that John spent in Adannaya's village, which was the last leg of his two-year missionary trip to Africa, seemed to fly by. While it was true the days were filled with work that was hard in such a hot, dry place, it was the nights that made the trip fulfilling.

The nights were filled with tribal dancing, exotic foods, celebration, and joy. And of course, there was also Adannaya.

In those six weeks, Adannaya became everything to John. Her smile, her joy, her acceptance of life and others touched him in ways he couldn't explain. What he did know, however, was how much Adannaya's attitude changed him. His eyes were opened to things he never truly saw before. Suddenly, what had previously looked bleak or hopeless now had new life. Who he once saw as just strangers he now saw as other human beings. He realized that every one of us is in this life together and people cannot only be here for themselves; rather, we must realize we are all here for each other.

Two days before he and his team went back to America, John did something he knew would change his life forever. "Adannaya, would you do me the honor of being my wife and coming back to America with me? I know this may seem sudden, but you have opened my eyes to so much beauty and changed my life in so many ways that I know in my heart I've fallen in love with you and want to be with you forever."

"Oh John, I don't know what to say. Are you sure about this? Is it possible you feel this way because you're in this place that is strange to you and when you get back home, you'll understand that you weren't really thinking? And I have my father and mother to think about. My sisters and everyone else. How can I just leave them? Oh John, I don't know."

"Please, just promise me you'll think about it over the next few days. Will you do that? Please?"

"I'll think about it, but I just don't know. Are you really sure about this?"

"I've never been more sure of anything in my life, Adannaya. You have opened my eyes and heart to what true love means."

"I just don't know, John. What will Father say? What will my family and the people of my village say? What will your family and the other people of your country say...?"

CHAPTER 16

"Didn't your great-grandparents live here?" Gavin asked Susan's mom.

"Yes, for most of their lives. But right after they were married and came to this country and my great-grandfather was asked to leave the ministry, the first place they moved to was New York City. They thought they'd feel like they'd belong there more than anywhere because there were so many people living there. Which led them to believe no one would notice a white man and black woman were together. And even if people did notice, my great-grandparents figured with all of those other people around, no one would care. And while it was true people there went about their own business, my great-grandparents tired of city life pretty quickly and moved right here to this town."

"Did they like living here? Did you know them?" Suddenly, Gavin could feel the mood lighten a little. Maybe there was some semblance of hope for him and his being different. After all, if Susan's mom's great-grandparents survived here, then maybe so could he if people found out his secret. But, as he was about to learn, that hope was short-lived.

"No, I never knew my great-grandparents, but I was told the real problems about being accepted started after they moved here. The discrimination against them must have been terrible, crosses burned on their lawn, windows smashed in their house. From what I was told, it was just awful. Sure, people seemed to accept my great-grandfather, but my great-grandmother was never welcomed in any way, shape, or form. She was treated like a disease; nobody wanted anything to do with her. At least, that is what I was told by my grandmother. My grandmother would say even she never felt like she belonged. When my grandmother was born, even the minister of their church refused to baptize her. And when she grew up, they quickly discovered none of the other children wanted to play with her or be her friend. School was terrible, she just hated it because she was always picked on and teased. Kids would say things like, 'Your momma's a blackie, your momma's a blackie...' I can't imagine it. I guess I really don't want to."

"If it was so terrible here, why did they stay?"

"According to what my grandmother told me, my great-grandmother wanted to leave; she absolutely hated it here, but my great-grandfather wouldn't hear of it. Apparently, his parents lived here and they were getting older and needed his help in managing things."

"So, his parents were all right with it even though no one else was?"

"Not completely. They never really accepted my great-grandmother, but my great-grandfather was their son and they wouldn't turn their back on one of their children, no matter who he was with. Not like so many people today. Look how many parents disown their own child because of who that child loves, whether it's a person of a different race or a person of the same sex. It might just be my opinion, and others may think it's silly, but what I can't understand is, why does it matter so much who your child loves? They're still your child no matter what, aren't they? And what I really don't understand is how those very same parents try to justify their actions by proclaiming what their child is doing goes against God. Did God ever turn His back on His son for reaching out in love to all others, like talking to the Samaritan woman or healing the leper? Did God turn His back on Jesus for teaching everyone to 'love your neighbor as yourself?' I don't think Jesus meant for us to just love the neighbors that look, act, and live like we do and forget about everybody else."

"But it's been like that for years, hasn't it?" Gavin asked. "I mean, look at what we're learning about the Civil War and how blacks were treated by whites. Some people seem so proud of the way slaves were treated but my question is, what was to be proud of? Why do some people try to use history to justify their mindsets and actions today? Why isn't the response a feeling of shame because of the actions of past generations and a vow to not bring that narrow-mindedness into society today? What is it that makes it okay to be prejudiced and dismissive toward another, no matter who that other is?"

"I thought we were past all of that too, but I guess I was wrong. I just don't understand it and I guess I never will," Susan's mom replied.

After what seemed like an hour, Susan came running down the stairs.

"Hey, Susan, want to go for a bike ride?"

"Sure, sounds like fun. What's up? Where should we ride to?"

"Oh, I don't know. Maybe just around town. There's something I want to talk to you about."

"Okay. Sounds important. Everything okay?" Susan said in mock seriousness.

"I guess. I don't know. I hope it will be after we talk."

"I'm sure everything will be fine."

"Maybe not after you hear what I tell you."

"God, you're such a worrywart. Everything will be fine, trust me."

"I do trust you, that's why I want to talk to you about it. Actually, you're the only one I do trust to tell."

Maybe it was because it was the end of summer, or maybe it was just because of the weather, but regardless of the reason it was one of those rare, glorious summer days when the temperature is just right and the wind plays softly across the back of your neck. The sky was a blue like neither one of them had ever seen, and all seemed right with the world. At least for the moment. But what would happen to Gavin's world once his secret was out? Would the clouds come? Would the sky turn black and the storms hit? That was the fear that had been lurking inside of him, constantly eating away any semblance of confidence he may have so valiantly tried to build up to face this moment.

To add to his fear was the fact that this was a small town. Summer in Napier Springs is, by experience, hot and humid. When one walks outside on most summer days, it feels like a hot, damp towel has been thrown over their head. While that in and of itself is enough to make one's summer an unbearable time, living in such a small town with nothing to do only makes summer that much worse, especially for a kid. For while it is true the first few weeks of summer vacation are a time of feeling free of the routine of lessons and homework, by the third week, summer becomes a time of boredom and idleness and trying to invent fun becomes tedious for most kids. Sure, video games help, but what parent would allow their child to sit endlessly in front of a screen trying to defend the world against evil or score points killing a zombie?

"There's too much living to do to waste it on video games."

"Go ride a bike; go play hide and seek; go play with your friends."

"Why not make some new friends, expand your horizons?"

"Why, I remember when I was a kid…"

Good Lord, how many times had Gavin heard those words from his parents?

Further, while the town is quaint in its own right, as most towns the size of Napier Springs are, and while it is true most people who live there know each other's names, there is a reality that exists that can make one feel excluded in a very real way. All one need do is pay close attention to what is being said, listen to the idle gossip to know there is a definitive layer of prejudice brought about by preconception that guides the mindsets and opinions of the people of Napier Springs.

The frightening thing is, this mindset is proudly shared from parent to child and has been for generations.

"Well in my day we would never..."

"All are this... and every one of those is that...and I wouldn't trust any one of them; actually, who could after seeing how they live their lives..."

And heaven help the child that doesn't adopt the same mindset as that of their parents or other people who live there. If a child has a different viewpoint or what is labeled as a "progressive idea" about life, they don't really belong. Sure, they exist in that place, but they can't really "live" there, live in the sense that they are fully free to be who they are. Living in Napier Springs is only for the right kind of people with the right kind of ideas and age-old systems of belief no matter their age; all others are doomed to exist in quiet solitude knowing they will never truly fit in or be accepted. After all, "those freakazoids" belong with their own kind, they don't belong with us."

And forget about ever being fully accepted if you are an "outsider" moving into this town—it just isn't going to happen. Because sadly even owning a house and paying property taxes, going to church every Sunday, or going to the annual town carnival or any other event held in Napier Springs will never be enough to fully erase the differences that exist in the people's minds and ultimately their hearts. Judgmental, dismissive, and discriminatory mindsets had been ingrained for far too many years for them to change now. The wall of preconception that is built in the mind and around the heart is too impenetrable for true acceptance or true love for the outsider.

As a result, the town is literally dying, with the apparent decline and decay happening there steadily marching forward. But in order to save it from what surely is its inevitable fate, which is something that is very apparent to most of the people of the town of Napier Springs, the town must reverse course, stop the onslaught of death resulting from the freefall of decline it currently finds itself in by recognizing and cherishing the differences that exist in life, and allowing real change to take place there. Unfortunately, the town's depressed state doesn't seem to matter much to most of the people who live there. All that seems to matter is hanging onto some unwritten but staunchly practiced mindset. If the town's demise is inevitable, then so be it. At least it won't be tainted because of the acceptance of something or someone so heinous, so sinful, so…

"Hey, kids, goin' for a bike ride?"

"Hi, Dad, you're home early," Susan said.

"Hi, honey, hi, Gavin. Yeah, I got finished early for a change, and instead of staying and starting another project, I figured I'd come home. Got some chores around here that I need to get done, like cutting the grass."

Mr. and Mrs. Williams have lived in Napier Springs their entire lives. It is the place they call home. The place where they are raising a family of four girls. The place that never seems to change—and as a result of not changing, never seems to grow.

CHAPTER 17

"Hello, Mrs. Richardson? My name is Pastor Todd Edwards. I'm with your son," turning toward him I ask in a whispered voice, "What is your name?"

"Gavin. My name is Gavin," he replies.

Turning back to the phone I say, "Please try to remain calm when I tell you Gavin was beaten up and is hurt."

"Beaten up? Who would beat him up and why would they do that? Who did you say you are? Why are you with my son? Can I talk to him? Why didn't you call an ambulance?"

"Try to calm down, ma'am, he's right here. Your mom wants to talk to you."

"Hi, Mom."

"Oh, honey, are you all right? What happened?"

"Some guys from school were beating on me."

"That's what the man on the phone told me. Why were they beating you up? Did you provoke them in some way? Are you badly hurt? Who is the man you are with? Why is he there?"

"No, Mom, I didn't provoke them. The guy who is with me is a minister. He saw that I was in trouble and stopped to help me. I guess his wife is hurt and they were on their way to the hospital and he thinks I should go with them and get checked out."

"Why would anyone beat you up? I don't understand, especially if you didn't provoke them."

Gavin suddenly feels his world start to crumble a little bit. Would he, by trying to explain to his mom what happened and why it happened, be opening the floodgates to the truth? Would his secret finally come out to his parents? And if it did, what would their reaction be? How could he hide it now? He needs to talk to his mom, he needs her to know, he needs her comfort, he needs her love. He so desperately needs her. Besides, if his friend Susan accepted him for who he is, why wouldn't his parents? They are supposed to love him no matter what, aren't they? But what if instead they hate him because of it? God, this is so hard.

"Let me talk to the man who is with you."

"Here, my mom wants to talk to you again," Gavin says as he hands the phone back to me.

"Yes, Mrs. Richardson, I'm back."

"How do I know you really are who you say you are? How do I know you're not just some freak who has my son?"

"Again, ma'am, please try to calm down. After all, if I was some freak, why would I call you in the first place?"

"My son said you are a minister. If that's true, what church do you preach at, and is there someone there who can verify it? What's the phone number so I can call them?"

"Look, Mrs. Richardson, the church office is closed, so no one is there right now. I serve the United in Christ church. I have my wife in the car with me. I was taking her to the emergency room because she cut herself and needs stitches. If it would help to make you feel better, I can put her on the phone, and you can talk to her. As a matter of fact, you can stay on the phone with her the entire time until we get to the hospital. Would that help you to feel better? Please believe me when I tell you I just want what is best for your son. My wife and I saw your son in trouble and stopped to help. I don't mean to sound rude, but the longer we have this conversation, the more time it will take me to get your son to the emergency room and possibly the help he needs."

"What hospital are you taking him to? My husband and I will be right there. I'm trusting you are who you say you are."

"Your mom said she and your father would meet us at the hospital emergency room; they are leaving right now," I say to Gavin as I put my phone back into my pocket.

"So, Mr. Minister, what made you feel different when you were my age?"

"We'll talk about that, but first thing is to get you two looked at by a doctor. Let's go."

CHAPTER 18

"Well, we're here," I say cheerily.

"Finally. I didn't think we'd ever make it," my wife replies moodily.

"How's the hand?"

"It hurts, that's how it is."

"Still?"

"Yes, still. What did you think it was going to do, magically heal on our way here?"

"I didn't say that." Unlike I had hoped, it is obvious my wife's mood isn't getting better.

"And how are you, Son?" I ask Gavin. "We'll have both of you looked at to make sure everything is okay, and then we'll be on our way. Shouldn't take too long."

"I'm achy, but I'm feeling okay. I don't know why I'm even here. I wonder if my parents are here yet?" Gavin replies.

"They might be sitting inside waiting for us."

As we enter the crowded emergency room, we immediately know we are facing a long night.

"Yeah right, 'shouldn't take long.' Look at this place—all of these people," my wife says sarcastically.

"Just relax, honey, we won't be long. I promise. Come on, let's get you two over to the registration desk."

"God, my hand hurts. I really didn't think I cut it this badly."

The registration desk is in the middle of the room surrounded by what have to be at least twenty people with various kinds of injuries or illnesses. Others who have already registered, what appear to be about one hundred people, are sitting in chairs scattered around the large room. In fact, there are so many people in the emergency room tonight there aren't even three chairs together for us to sit in. This is going to take hours, no doubt about that.

After we finally register and receive our number to be called when it is our turn to be treated, we head to a quiet corner of the room away from the crowd. Even though we will have to stand or sit on the floor, at least we will be able to relax together until it is our turn.

T.V.s hanging on the walls around the room show images from a news channel with closed captions because hearing what the news anchors are saying is next to impossible. In a far corner there is a small play area set up with toys for children, who largely ignore it, and instead stick close to their parents.

"Good Lord, look at all of these people! We're going to be here all night and this cut on my hand is killing me. Brilliant call bringing us here, genius, let me tell you. I could have just as easily bled to death at home in peace and quiet."

"You weren't going to bleed to death. I wouldn't have let that happen. We'll be seen in no time, you'll see."

"Yeah, right, 'no time' will take all night. Then who will see?" my wife says condescendingly.

"Patience, dear, patience; I promise you, it's not going to take all night."

"You can't promise me anything," is her response.

Over an intercom, a voice can be heard calling out, "Number seventeen! Patient number seventeen will now be seen!"

"What number are we?" my wife asks me.

"We are number sixty-eight."

"Oh, nice, only fifty-one away. Like I said, this is going to take all night."

According to a television news channel that is playing, there was another random shooting. It is being reported that at least twenty people are dead, and dozens were wounded.

"Look at that, more senseless violence. Another shooting somewhere."

"Where?"

"According to news reports, very near here."

"What happened?"

"I don't know, I'm trying to read what the reporters are saying. It looks like someone walked into a crowded pizza restaurant and opened fire. The police suspect it was racially motivated. It looks like someone was angry about something and was looking to get revenge. Good Lord, what is happening to this world? It's like all that matters is hate, hate, hate..."

"I guess that would explain why all of these people are here. God, I wish my hand would stop hurting."

"It's awful how some people just go shooting up places and don't care who they hurt or kill. I often wonder what makes a person do that. It makes no sense whatsoever," I say.

CHAPTER 19

"So, why weren't you accepted when you were my age?" Gavin asks me.

"Good Lord, that was a long time ago. To be honest, I don't think I'd remember."

"But you said you felt the same way when you were my age. So, you lied to me? If you don't think you can remember when you were my age, how do you know how you felt? A minister lied to me. God, why did I ever listen to you? Who the hell are you? Where are my parents? I need to find my parents. I need to get out of here."

"First off, I'm someone who cares about you, that's who I am. And secondly, no, I didn't lie to you. I said I probably felt the same way you do now when I was your age, and the reality is I probably did. That was not a lie."

"What's your wife's name again?"

"Her name is Ann. Why?"

"Excuse me, Ann, do you think you can help me find my parents? I need to get away from this lying husband of yours."

"Whoa, hold on there, sport, I told you I didn't lie to you. And no one is going looking for anyone else right now," I say to Gavin. "There are way too many people in here for you to just go wandering off on your own. When your parents come, we'll hook up with them.

Just stand right there and keep your eye on that door, and you'll be able to see when they walk in. Besides, I thought you wanted to hear my story."

"I thought you just said you don't remember your story. So probably all I'm going to hear coming out of your mouth is a bunch of bullshit to try to make me feel better. Hell, I wouldn't be surprised if you make it up as you go along, so I'll keep my mouth shut."

"Whoa kid, watch your mouth. Now, do you want to hear my story or not?"

"If it's a lie, no, I don't want to hear it."

"How many times do I have to tell you it's not a lie? Okay, tell you what, I'll tell you my story from the last fifteen years; that much I can remember. How will that be? Will that be okay with you?"

"Whatever. I don't really care at this point. Do what you want."

"He always does, believe me. I've been married to him for twenty-seven years now," my wife says to Gavin.

"Hey, whose side are you on?" I ask my wife. Turning to Gavin I say, "What's it going to be kid, either you want to hear it or you don't."

"Yeah, whatever."

"Not whatever. It's either yes or no—pick one."

Looking toward my wife, Gavin asks her, "What do you think? Think I should let him tell it?"

"He'll tell it to you whether you want to hear it or not."

"I will not. It's completely up to him. But I think it will help him to hear it."

"Yeah, why do you say that? How will my hearing your story help me in any way?" Gavin asks me.

"Because I think it will show you that you are not alone and that you really do belong here. Weren't you the one who said, 'I shouldn't even be alive?' Well, I'm here to tell you that's a load of BS, forgive my boldness. You are here for a very specific reason. We all are. At least that's what I believe. Why, considering what I went through in just the last fifteen years, I should have walked away from ministry, but as you can see, I didn't. It was made perfectly clear by those in authority that I didn't belong, but did that stop me?"

"No, I guess not, 'cause you're still a minister. At least on the outside. But what about on the inside? Is your heart still in it? Do you feel like you belong in ministry?"

"Good questions, kid. Obviously it didn't stop him, but like I've asked him hundreds of times, where did his staying in ministry get us? You ask him to tell you the answer to that question. I know I'd like to hear the answer," my wife responds.

"Okay, Mr. Minister, you felt like you didn't belong but you stuck it out anyway. So, like your wife said, where did it get you? Huh?"

"Actually, it's gotten me pretty far because it's given me a new appreciation for who I am. It's given me the opportunity to embrace my shortcomings or disabilities or whatever you want to call them and celebrate me for who I am. No, it may not have gotten me riches or financial success. It actually may have made the pursuit of those things that much more difficult. But in the end when I do attain it, and I will attain it, I will have come to appreciate it even more because I will have fully accepted me. And when that happens, I'll no longer have to play the puppet on the string dancing to another's will, trying to become who they want me to become because it's uncomfortable for them when I'm not. Are they willing to dance on my string because they aren't like me? The obvious answer is no. So, if everyone goes around trying to change everyone else to fit their idea of what comfort around others should look like, what will we end up with? Experiences outside of our comfort zone are a great teacher, Son." I continue, "They not only push us to be more than we think we could possibly be, they actually become a part of us. They change a person. Why, they even determine how we live our lives, how we not only see ourselves, but everyone else as well. And believe me, I've had my share of experiences..."

Immediately my mind goes back to my first day of seminary...

CHAPTER 20

"Welcome to your first day with us at Trinity Evangelical Seminary. While there are many things we need to go over in order to make your learning experience with us enriching and fulfilling, one of the first things we need to talk about is that in order to graduate, each of you is required to participate in some type of ministerial or mission-oriented program. That can either be a hands-on experience in a nursing home type setting or a cross-cultural trip where you are immersed in the local culture of that particular country working as a missionary. The choice will be yours, but it is required of every student. And even though there are a number of local options you can choose from, there is only one cross-cultural missionary experience, and this year it is to South Africa. If you decide you want to go on the cross-cultural trip, we will need to know by the end of this week so we can finalize arrangements."

South Africa? The cross-cultural trip this year is to South Africa? As I sat in that classroom surrounded by the other students, all I could think about was how I'd always wanted to go to Africa. The people, the animals, the colors, the landscape. I'd always been fascinated by Africa; watching all of those animal shows when I was a kid, looking through nature magazines, imagining I was on safari or was some famous African explorer. And now all of these years later, I have the chance to experience first-hand what I could only imagine before. "No matter the cost, I'm going," I say to myself...

Gavin's voice suddenly snaps me back to the present moment. "Yeah right, you've had your share of experiences. What experiences have you had that could help me in any way?"

"Well, for one, I went to South Africa and experienced what life was like there for people."

"Big deal, so you went to Africa. What do I care?"

"Maybe my going to Africa is no big deal to you, but it wasn't just in the going. It was what I found there that changed me."

"So, what? What did you find there? Probably nothin' more than a bunch of animals, and did going to Africa to look at animals change you that much? Besides, how does your going to Africa help me in any way?"

"Actually, that was my initial opinion of Africa. As far as I knew or even thought, Africa was only animals and safaris. But after I met the people who lived there, I realized that I had only been looking at Africa on a shallow surface level. And that wasn't fair. The thing is, even though I didn't know it at the time, after experiencing the peoples of South Africa first hand I came to understand that by my just looking at Africa on a shallow surface level, I was being most unfair to myself. There is no way to fully grow as a person by remaining shallow. And I'm not talking about growing physically. I'm talking about growing emotionally."

"Hey, why not remain shallow? It's safer that way. Why should I care about growing emotionally? Why should anybody, for that matter?"

"That's a fair question. Let's see if we can find an answer that you're comfortable with. The people of Africa are incredible. At least the ones that I met."

"Yeah right, what's so incredible about the people who live in Africa? Far as I care, they're nothin' but a bunch of savages..."

"Hm, savages. That's an interesting but very common view of how others see them," I replied. And then my mind began to drift once again...

CHAPTER 21

As I sat in the plane early that morning ready to take off for a land that to me was foreign and strange, although I felt excitement, my mind was filled with thoughts of Africa and my heart was filled with fear. I was afraid of so many things. Things that were new and unfamiliar. I had never been on an airplane before in my life, and now I was about to fly across an ocean to a place I'd so far only dreamt about. But when I got there, what would I find? Sure, I knew the people that I was traveling to Africa with because they were in my class. But even though they were classmates, they were still strangers to me. To be perfectly honest, I really didn't know much about their lives and they didn't know much about mine. To add to my anguish was the fact that my wife and son weren't going with me, so I was pretty much on my own.

A further fear that weighed heavy upon my mind was the question, "What will the people who live there be like?" I didn't speak their language, I didn't live like they did, so my life, I imagined, was totally different than theirs. Maybe on a surface level that is a truth, but deep down inside, where it really matters, reality shows us none of us are different at all. Ever think to yourself, how in God's name will I ever fit into that landscape? Will those people accept me even though I am only going to be a part of their lives for a very short period of time? What if they only see me as some foreigner invading their lives? How will they understand me and how will I understand them?

And then the question sprang into my head: what am I doing? On the surface it sounded so romantic, so exciting, but thinking about it, was it really? Or was this going to turn out to be some kind of nightmare that I would be better off waking up from now?

"Ladies and gentlemen, welcome aboard Flight 178 with service from New York to Johannesburg, South Africa. We are currently fourth in line for takeoff and are expecting to be in the air in approximately ten minutes. We ask that you please make sure your seat belts are fastened and all baggage is secure underneath the seat in front of you or in the overhead compartments. We also ask that your seats and table trays are in an upright position. Please turn off all laptops and please put your cell phones in Airplane mode. Our flight will last approximately seventeen hours and smoking is prohibited the entire duration of the flight. Thank you for choosing Kumzalwane Airlines and enjoy your flight. Currently it is raining and there is a storm moving through the area, so we could have a bumpy take off. Our cruising altitude will be 37,000 feet. Again, thank you for choosing Kumzalwane Airlines and enjoy your flight. If you are in need of anything during the duration of the flight, our stewards and stewardesses are here to assist you."

As soon as I heard that announcement I knew there was no turning back. I was headed straight for whatever lay across the ocean. I was about to experience something that was totally strange. Would I accept it or would I judge it? Was I actually judging it already based on fear and perception and didn't realize it...?

Coming back to the present moment and looking at Gavin, I continue, "The people there are incredible. They have this joy about them that is infectious. Even though the circumstances they live under are unimaginably horrible and the poverty they live under would be unbearable for us, they are the happiest people I have ever seen in my life. The houses they live in are nothing more than these four-foot by eight foot corrugated tin shacks with dirt floors, and there might be a family of four to six people living there. No running water, only communal wells and toilets—no electricity, no privacy, and yet they are filled with this sense of joy and acceptance that is infectious. I'll never forget this one church we went to." I continue, "Even though it was January, they knew the Americans were coming, and they wanted to keep their Christmas decorations up for us to see and enjoy. You know what their decorations were?"

"How would I know?" Gavin says, rather sarcastically. "I'm sure a Christmas tree and, being a church, probably a manger scene."

"That's what anyone else, including I, would think too. But their only Christmas decoration was an eighteen-inch piece of tinsel garland thumbtacked to a wall. That was it, nothing else because they were too poor to afford anything else. Actually, one of the parishioners told us he found it in a dumpster and brought it to the church, otherwise there wouldn't have been any Christmas decorations. Now just think about that for a moment. It was found in a dumpster, and yet they were proud of it. How proud are we to show off something we may have found in a dumpster, or do we make fun of those who go 'dumpster diving?' Do we consider people who do that poor and pathetic?"

"I don't know...probably...whatever. So, if they're so poor that they have to go dumpster diving, what makes them so happy?"

"I'm glad you asked me that. What makes them so happy is that they have each other. Not only that, but they genuinely love and respect each other and that is all they need. Anything else that comes into their lives they consider to be a bonus. They don't need the latest or greatest, all they need is each other."

"Well, good for them, but they're in Africa and we're in the USA. People here are different," Gavin replies.

"How are they different?" I ask. "True, the people who live in Africa have different desires than we do and their mindsets and beliefs are different, but aren't people, people, no matter who they are or where they live? Their environment might be different, and their circumstances might not be the same as ours, but they are still people nonetheless, aren't they?"

"Yeah, they're people, but they don't look at life like we do."

"Number one, how do you know that for sure? Don't they feel disappointment like we do? Don't they laugh or cry like any other human being does? Are they not just as fit to live as you or I, or anyone else we may know, no matter their circumstances or desires? So no, they may not look at life like you or I do but so what, why do they have to? And number two, why can't they see life the way they see it and that's good enough for us? They aren't hurting anyone, are they? Yeah, if they were terrorizing or destroying or killing then I'd be the first to speak out against them and their actions, but they're not, so why judge them?"

"I'm not. Hell. I don't even know them."

"That's very true, you don't know them. So, let me ask; how many people in this country are there that you don't you know personally but you judge anyway?"

"I don't judge anybody else."

"Really? Are you sure?"

"Yeah, I'm sure."

"Okay, prove it. Take that person sitting over there."

"Which person?"

"The one sitting over there by the table," I reply.

"You mean the poor guy or the other one?" Gavin asks.

"How do you know one guy is poor and the other one is not? Do you know either of them?"

"No, I don't know them."

"Then how do you know one is poor?"

"Look at how he is dressed: ripped jacket, dirty pants, shoes with holes in them."

"But if you don't know that person, how do you know he is poor? Maybe he is quite well off and just chooses to dress that way."

"I don't think anyone with money would chose to dress like that."

"Why not?"

"Look at him; he looks like a slob."

"So just because he looks like a slob to you then he must be poor? Is it fair to feel that way about someone you don't know?"

"Okay, so maybe he's not poor, but he sure looks like he is, even you can't deny that."

"This has nothing to do with me acknowledging or denying anything. What it does have to do with is really seeing. Just because someone looks a certain way doesn't necessarily mean they are that way, does it?"

"No, I guess not," Gavin replies.

"So, isn't basing our opinion on someone's outside appearance being judgmental? Just because a chameleon changes its outer appearance does that mean it changes who it is."

Gavin just looks at me.

"It works the same for people. Just because someone appears to us to be one way on the outside doesn't mean that's who they really are, does it?"

"Whatever. To me it's just pointing out what I see."

"But how is it fair to the other person to determine their value based only upon how we see them and not what we actually know about them? Or are you saying we don't have to consider the entire person, inside and out?"

I continue, "Like you, you don't like it when the other kids only look at your outside and don't even consider what makes you tick, do you?"

"No, I don't think that's fair."

"And you feel it's not fair because you feel you are being judged based only upon one part of you?"

"Yeah, that's not fair," he replies.

"Well, guess what kid? We all do it; judge others. But just because we can and do judge, does that make it right? Again, take yourself as an example; you told me kids that don't fully know you judge you, right?"

"Yeah, I guess so."

"What do you mean you guess so? You know so, don't you?"

"Yeah, I know I'm judged," Gavin replies angrily.

"And you know by who, right?"

"Yeah, I know by who."

"Well, how does that make you feel, and are you okay with that?"

"Look, I already told you I'm not okay with it. It makes me feel like shit. What are you, stupid or something?"

"No, I'm not 'stupid or something', I'm just trying to understand something here. So, let me get this straight, you don't think it's fair that you are being judged by the other kids in school, right?"

"I already said it's not fair."

"Why not?"

"Because they don't really know who I am. They don't know how I feel about things and it's like they don't even care. It's like they think they are these chosen kids that everyone should bow down to, listen to what they say, and let them do whatever they want to do and to hell with what anyone else feels or says. It's not right and it's not fair.

I mean who do they think they are anyway, these perfect kids who everyone should look up to?"

"Well, do you really know them? Sure, you see their outside actions and behavior, but what about what's going on inside of their heads and hearts? What if they really feel insecure about themselves for some reason unknown to you?"

"Why should I care about what they think or feel? I know how they'd feel about me because I see how they act now towards me and the other kids who aren't like them, and I don't like it. Why should I anyway? You probably wouldn't."

"So, you don't like how they act so you judge them by those actions?"

"Yeah, I judge them by their actions."

"So, you just admitted you judge, and you think that's fair."

"Yeah, I think it's fair, why wouldn't I?"

"Because aren't you doing to them the exact same thing they are doing to you?"

"What are you talking about? I'm not doin' nothin'."

"Yeah, actually you are. Like I said, we all do."

"What am I doin'?"

"You're judging someone based only upon how you see them, not on what you know about them."

"So what?"

"So, it doesn't bother you that you're merely judging on outside appearance or actions?"

"No, it doesn't; why should it?"

"Because isn't that hypocritical of you? You don't like to be judged by others who don't really know you, but it's okay for you to judge those you don't really know?"

"Why is that hypocritical? Like you said, everybody does it, including you."

"But just because we can do something doesn't make it right when we do it, does it?" I ask.

"Whatever."

Ed. D'Agostino

CHAPTER 22

Without challenging experiences, where would any one of us be? Don't the experiences we live through make us who we are? Do they not add multiple dimensions to what would otherwise be a one dimensional and boring life? And while it is true not every experience is a pleasant one, guess what, they're not supposed to be, because if they were, think about how soft you would be. If everything in your life was easy and carefree, imagine how spoiled and self-centered you'd end up becoming, never empathizing with those who are not like you and do not live your lifestyle?

Yet when we look at another, including the stranger, what do we see? Is it two eyes like we have? Do they have two arms like we do? Do they stand up and sit down like we do? Do they have a nose and ears like we do? In other words, do we simply assign value based solely upon outside appearances, like if someone is black or white, male or female, tall or short, thin or fat? Or must we take deeper issues into account? Issues like traditions and beliefs and lifestyles and political leanings?

Thomas Kempis wrote, "Love feels no burden, thinks nothing of its trouble, attempts what is above its strength, pleads no excuse for impossibility, for it thinks all things are lawful for itself, and all things are possible."

Is belonging to the entire world possible? Can anyone expect to be accepted, let alone loved, by everyone else on earth or is that just an amusing fantasy? Is the world just too big, cultures too diverse, and belief systems too entrenched for there to be any hope for someone to fully belong with all others? While it might be a nice dream to think the possibility exists, is that all it is, a dream, a fallacy? Isn't it a huge waste of time to think about how incredible this planet would be if that dream became a reality?

Besides, what does it mean to belong anyway? For even though it does provide each of us with some measure of comfort, does belonging expand our possibilities?

Maya Angelou said, "I do not trust people who don't love themselves and yet tell me, 'I love you.' There is an African saying which is: be careful when a naked man offers you a shirt." Is it possible to love the one we do not trust, or is trust the foundation upon which love is built? Is fully and faithfully belonging in the world just a matter of being accepted by others, including the stranger? Or for someone to feel like they fully belong, must they first accept themselves for who they are? Must one be comfortable with who he or she is no matter lifestyle, political party affiliation, economic class…? Must one, from his or her own perspective, see they have value in order for others, including the stranger, to be comfortable with and accepting of them? Have you ever asked yourself any of these questions? And if your answer to any of them is yes, then the next question you must ask yourself is, how do you express that answer to show others belonging is an action and not just a word?

If, on the other hand, you answer no, what needs to change in your mindset, or do you believe your mindset is just fine the way it is and nothing needs to change? And is it just your mindset, or are there other things in your life that must change as well? "If others don't have to accept me then I have every right not to accept another as well." Have you ever felt that way? If the answer to that is yes, is that feeling selfish and selfishness is the real problem? "If they don't have to I don't have to either...If I can't have things my way, I don't have to accept their way either...If I get hurt by someone, I have every right to hurt another...If they did it, then so can I."

Throughout my life I've come to the conclusion there are many things humans are good at. Truth is, we all have the ability to do a variety of things. Just think about all the things we do every day—and of course, we all know how true it is that there are some things we are better at doing than others.

Consider how some people are good at sports and others are good at cooking or math or art, medicine, crafts or this, that, or the other thing. So, what about you; what are you good at? If I ask one hundred people, I'd probably get one hundred different answers.

Unfortunately, there is one thing each and every one of us can do equally well without much training or long hours of practice. What is that, you might ask.

The answer is: discriminate against others.

Discrimination comes so easily to us. It's like it is nothing more than just some natural extension of our lives and so it's no big deal when we discriminate. Discrimination has become such an ordinary part of our lives that judgmental words simply roll off of our tongues and our discriminatory actions appear to be nothing more than second-nature.

The truth is, discriminating mindsets are actually a learned behavior. They are actions that we have experienced personally that have developed into some kind of selfish justification, or they are actions we have witnessed coming from someone we have looked up to like a parent, guardian, or some other type of authoritative figure. But because they are learned actions, the good news is we can unlearn them. We can overcome them if we want to.

Unfortunately, these behaviors have become so commonplace in our everyday lives that many have come to some misplaced conclusion they don't have the time to change them because they are too busy with more important matters. Or isn't ridding ourselves of discriminatory and judgmental actions and mindsets really about a lack of time? Is it simply a fact that we have no desire to even want to change them because we believe there is nothing to overcome, we believe we are fine just as we are, and it's "those others" that are messed up?

However, and whether or not we realize it, in order to survive and move forward in any successful way those things which we've learned, and continue to learn throughout life, we must be open to change and progression, including mindsets and behaviors. For if we hold onto what we were taught only in the ways in which we were taught them, how could we as a species ever progress?

Take the lion, for example. His hunting territory is consistently decreasing in size, so he must adapt those ways in which he was taught to hunt to meet the demands of the current situation in which he finds himself. Because if he instead insists upon clinging to some narrow mindset of 'this is the way I've always hunted…' he will surely starve to death. So it is with any of us and all of the lessons we may learn.

How often in life have I witnessed people rallying around each other in times of disaster? I see it happening right now with the hurricanes that devastated so many different places and affected so many people. Volunteers from every race, religious background, and lifestyle are working together to help those adversely affected by the storm. And if we admit it, the truth is we've all seen how freely the emotion we call love is expressed and uncompromisingly shared with victims of any and all major tragedies.

And while one might call it hands-on support or financial assistance or whatever words one uses to justify their outreach and make it more palatable to them, the fact of the matter is, no matter what you call it, it is still a form of love. But is it all right to restrict our love for the stranger to only times when tragedy befalls them? In those events the sharing of that emotion is acceptable, but at all other times it is nothing more than some imagined weakness? Is that mindset not wrong? And if your answer is no, then why is it not wrong to take that emotion and make it small and narrow? Actually, why is it okay to take any emotion and restrict it by establishing boundaries, such as "I only cry at this time" or "I only laugh at that time," around it?

Why is it that we believe that a natural disaster, such as a flood or a tornado, should bring all people together, but then when the storms have passed, we give those very same people who helped the afflicted permission to go back to the mindset they previously held? Why is it when we need help we disregard the good Samaritan's religion, lifestyle, or politics, but when we are no longer in need, those things become foremost in determining our acceptance or rejection of them?

Further, if the media is fake or foolhardy in its reporting of the facts, why would weather forecasters share information about the destructive forces of a storm and urge people to evacuate areas most likely to feel the brunt of it if they don't care? Oh, that's right, they are only out to stir things up so they are trying to pass some kind of liberal agenda. Which means all weather forecasters are liberal trolls bowing to some liberal god of "bleeding hearts." And if that is the case now I'm really confused, because if this is all merely some kind of liberal game that is being played by the media, then why do conservative newscasters also take part in that game by reporting the same things?

And why is it okay to take facts and try to bend them to fit some kind of self-perceived fallacy? When factual evidence is placed in front of your eyes, why look blindly at it and discount its value by proclaiming it to be nothing more than hyperbole established by those who are not in agreement with your mindset or opinions? What I feel is a relevant example of this is the environment. If we, as a nation, do not move forward in the progression of environmental science and simply call its discoveries fake, what will happen?

I think of climate change in particular. Why is it decades of study and findings by experts in the field of environmental science and ecology are relegated to the dust bin of fake or made-up hyperbole, but the proclamations of a handful of those who have no experience in scientific research are branded as having expert opinions and speaking truth? Is it because of our fears? Is it because it is easier to ignore or deny climate change instead of changing our ways of living in order to be more proactive about saving the environment? Isn't it easier to call warnings about climate change "fake," that way we can devalue and denounce them, won't have to think about them, and can instead cling to doing things the way we've always done them? Hell, by devaluing and denouncing climate change we won't have to grow or change in any way.

Thing is, if we denounce and devalue things like climate change for our lives, we are also effectively doing the same for the lives of our children, grandchildren, and beyond, aren't we? And how fair is that, especially to the rights of the unborn?

CHAPTER 23

Or what about other lessons we encounter every day?

Gavin looks at me and asks what is definitely a profound question: "If the teachings of Jesus are so sacred to you, Mr. Minister, and His self-proclaimed followers, what about His teaching to love your neighbors? How is supporting building a wall to keep our neighbors out showing them any kind of love? And I know what you're going to say; 'it's not to keep everyone out, just the illegals.' Well, let me ask you something, which ones are the illegals? What do they look like? Does it have to do with age? Is that it? Must one be a certain age in order to be considered an illegal?"

I stand there as Gavin continues, "How about the mother that comes to this country with her two children to escape abuse from either her spouse or the narrow-mindedness of her community or government, which of the three are illegal, just the mom, or are the kids illegal too?"

I must admit I am caught off guard and don't know how to answer him.

"The reality is age has no factor in this at all," Gavin continues. "It can't in order for the narrow-mindedness of statements like, 'Regardless of age, race, or nation, if someone is not born in this country they are illegal, period,' from this country's leadership to survive and grow. To hell with the fact they are my neighbors, right? I don't have to worry about them, right? Right, Mr. Minister? But yet didn't Jesus literally command all of his followers to love them? That's what the minister preaches at the church I go to with my family."

Again, silence from my side of the conversation.

Gavin is on a roll as he continues on. "Or how about closing off the borders, banning people from coming here, does that show love and acceptance, 'love thy neighbor,' or is that showing our neighbors something else? And before you answer, and regardless of your current age, put yourself on the other side of the wall or in the airport hearing the words, 'Sorry but you're not welcome here, I don't care how old or young you are...' Got that in mind? Now how do you feel? Not too good, huh?"

"No, I don't," I answer him.

"Then why is it okay for one of this country's greatest symbols of hope and peace, the Statue of Liberty, to proudly proclaim, 'Give me your tired, your poor, your huddled masses yearning to breathe free' but then a faction of this country's citizens, including its leadership, have no problem categorizing those from other countries yearning to breathe free as illegals? All that these supposed 'illegal aliens' are doing is trying to seize an opportunity to become more than they currently are, seize an opportunity to grow and learn."

"That may be so, but how many that come here really do try to cheat or steal or worse?" I say to Gavin.

"But that's my point. Just because there are those from other countries who try to 'play the system,' why is it okay to assume that every person from that country, including the kids, are terrorists or whatever the hell we label them and lump them all into one category by saying they are all this or that or the other thing so we're closing the borders to all of them? How is that fair?"

My mind immediately goes back to my earlier thought of the world going to hell in a handbasket, and I know he is right. How is it fair to lump an entire culture into a narrow mindset? It isn't. Yet how many of us do it anyway? And again, why do we do that? Is it only because of a fear of "what if" they are a terrorist, "what if" they are using their children to get into this country and they'll end up killing and maiming others, or is there more to it than some fear? And then the thought comes to me: is this just my country or does it belong to everyone who lives here, whether or not I know them or agree with them?

Does Christian teaching instruct its students to "close your minds, close your hearts, close your borders, turn your backs on those not like you..." or are Christians taught to "go into the world and make disciples of all nations"? If they close themselves off from the rest of the world, how will Christians ever be able to share the lessons Jesus taught or words He spoke? How will Christian principles, which this nation proclaims it was founded upon, be seen?

Or maybe the better question is, if the teachings of Christianity are things you profess not to believe nor follow then how about humanitarian teaching? After all, who reading this doesn't consider themselves to be a human being? And if everyone reading this says they are, then how can we as the human race justify building walls and closing borders to other human beings? And if we support building those walls and closing those borders because other countries have done it, what words, through our actions, will the peoples of the other nations of the world hear? What lessons will they learn? Are we really going to be seen as great again? And if so, who will see us that way? All others or selfishly only ourselves? Or does it only matter that we see ourselves as great and no one else in the world has to?

Nelson Mandela said, "As we let our own light shine we unconsciously give other people permission to do the same."

One of the biggest risks anyone can take, but one of the most rewarding wins they will ever enjoy, is when they accept themselves for who they are and no longer hide behind some self-imposed facade of supposed safety.

"Let me ask you something else; how do you feel about yourself?" I ask Gavin.

"Excuse me?"

"How do you feel about yourself? Are you okay with you for who you are, or have you not really accepted yourself and that's why you feel you have to hide who you really are? After all, like Mother Teresa once said and I quote, 'We think sometimes that poverty is only being hungry, naked, and homeless. The poverty of being unwanted, unloved, and uncared for is the greatest poverty. We must start in our own homes to remedy this kind of poverty.' So, let me ask you again; do you feel unloved and unwanted even in your own home?"

"What does that mean? Are you trying to be some kind of shrink or somethin'? Are you saying my parents don't love me?"

"I think what Mother Teresa is saying here is that we have to look into our own lives and see if we are taking care of ourselves and if we're not, then ask ourselves why not. Ask ourselves 'What's wrong with me that I don't accept me?' We must find the answer to that question first before we can truly accept and take care of anyone else. Because if we don't accept ourselves for who we are in our own homes," I say as I gesture toward my body, "why would we ever have the desire to truly consider anyone else in their 'homes?' And when we don't care about others and they don't care about us, that and not just the lack of financial security, is real poverty. So how about it, kid, do you accept yourself for who you are or don't you?"

"What, like I'm embarrassed about myself or something like that?"

"Are you embarrassed?"

"No, I'm not, and who the hell do you think you are asking me such a bullshit question?"

"Is it a lousy question or is it the truth?"

"No, it's not the truth."

"Okay, well I sure feel discriminated against by other people; how about you, do you feel discriminated against by anybody, including your parents? Apparently you must, otherwise you wouldn't feel like you have such a big secret to hide."

"You'd never understand it," Gavin says to me angrily. "And you never will."

"Oh, I think I understand you better than you think I do," I reply.

"You know what, I gotta get out of here, away from you." Looking at my wife, Gavin continues, "You know something, lady, your husband is a real piece of work, let me tell you. I don't know how you put up with his shit."

As he walks down the hall away from the emergency room, Gavin starts to replay the events of the day in his mind. Why does shit always happen to him? Why is he singled out to be bullied and tormented? Why don't people just leave him the hell alone, he doesn't bother any of them.

"Hello, young man. Is there something I can help you with or find?" a nurse asks him as he walks by.

"No thanks, I'm fine, I'm just taking a walk," Gavin replies.

"You know, visiting hours are over and you're not permitted in this part of the hospital after visiting hours."

"Oh sorry, I didn't know that. Is there someplace I can go where I can sit in quiet and think a little?"

"There's the chapel outside those doors and to the left, about halfway down the hall."

"Thanks, but no thanks, I don't want anything to do with God right now."

"You don't have to talk to God or pray or whatever; it's nice and quiet in there, you can just sit in silence and think if you like, nobody's going to bother you."

"Thanks, but really not interested."

"There's also the cafeteria. That's one floor down. It might not be as quiet as the chapel in there but you can get yourself a snack if you're hungry."

"Thanks, I am a little hungry. I think I'll try that. How do I get there?"

"Just go through those other doors over there, down the steps, turn right, and you'll come to it."

"Thanks again."

"My pleasure. You take care of yourself," says the nurse as she walks away.

"Okay, through those doors down the stairs and to the right; got it," Gavin says to himself.

When he reaches it, Gavin sees that the cafeteria is a lot larger than he has imagined. It looks a lot cleaner than the one he is used to in school as well. But it is still a cafeteria. However, as Gavin soon discovers, the food choices are a lot better.

After he makes his selections and pays for them, he finds an empty table near the back of the room and sits down.

As he sits there eating his slice of pizza, which isn't bad, especially for cafeteria food, the recent conversation creeps into his mind. "Just who the hell does Mr. Minister think he is, asking me if I'm embarrassed about myself? I've spent my entire life accepting who I am. So what if I hide it from everyone else? That doesn't mean I'm embarrassed, I'm just trying to protect myself from being made fun of, which is what everyone would do to me if they found out my secret. Nothing embarrassing about trying to protect yourself. I'm sure he'd do the same thing if he were in my shoes; anybody would.

Embarrassed, my ass. You know, this pizza's pretty good. I think I'll get another slice."

CHAPTER 24

Gavin's parents, Nancy and Ron, run into the emergency room, frantically searching for their son.

"Where is he? Where is my baby?" his mother says to his dad.

"I don't see him anywhere," replies her husband. "Let's go ask at the desk."

"Excuse me, have you seen our son? We received a phone call he was being brought here."

"I'll be with you in one moment, sir; as you can see, you are not the only ones here," the receptionist replies without hiding her sarcasm. *Can't people see I'm busy,* she thinks to herself. *Why does everyone think they are the only ones I have to deal with? God, I can't stand this place most days. I understand people who come in here are upset, but come on, give me a freakin' break already.*

"But you don't understand. I need to see my baby boy now."

"Ma'am please calm down, I will be right with you."

"While you're waiting here I'll search the waiting area. I'll be right back," Ron says to his wife.

As Ron quickly walks around the waiting room, he barely notices the faces of all of the other people sitting there. His mind is too consumed with finding his son. Who really cares about other people and their problems? They don't affect his life in any way. Besides, he has more important things to think about.

After what seems like an interminable time, the receptionist looks up from her computer screen and asks Nancy, "All right, ma'am, now how may I help you?"

"It's about time," Nancy says in exasperation. "My son. I need to see my son. I got a phone call from some minister that told me my son was beaten up and he was bringing him here. Have you seen them? Please tell me you've seen my son."

"Calm down, ma'am. There are a lot of people here right now; what does your son look like?"

"Oh God, please don't tell me my son was kidnapped; please tell me you've seen him. Please."

"Ma'am, calm down, you're getting hysterical here. We're going to find your boy. Now I'm going to ask you again, what does he look like?"

"He's about five feet, ten inches tall. He has dark hair, and he's skinny. I think too skinny, but he doesn't think so. Oh God, he's not too skinny, what am I saying? I need to see my baby. Here's a picture of him." Nancy shows the receptionist a picture she has of Gavin on her cell phone.

"Yes ma'am, I saw someone like that come through here about half an hour ago. With a middle-aged couple. Seemed like nice folks. The woman had a cut on her hand. They went over in that direction to find a seat," the receptionist replies, pointing to the left of the waiting area.

"Thank you, thank you so much. Ron, Gavin went over this way!" Nancy calls to her husband as she heads in the direction the receptionist pointed.

As Nancy scours the left side of the waiting area in search of her son, looking at the faces of all of the others there, she thinks to herself, *Good Lord, look at all of these people, so much anguish on some of their faces.* However, some have the appearance of being more bored than anything.

"Excuse me, are you Gavin Richardson's mom? I'm Pastor Todd Edwards, we spoke on the phone."

"Oh, thank God. Yes, I'm Gavin's mother, how is he? Where is he? Is he being examined by a doctor? Is he hurt badly?"

"Mrs. Richardson, your boy is going to be fine. No, he's not being examined by a doctor; actually I'm not sure where he went."

"What do you mean you don't know where he went? I thought he was with you? Where did he go? What have you done with my son?"

"We were talking, Gavin got angry, and he walked down that hall. I was just about to go looking for him when I saw you. If you'd like to come with me, that would be fine."

"Hell yes, I'm going with you. That's my baby boy you're talking about, how the hell could you just let him walk away like that? What the hell is the matter with you? God, he could be anywhere in this place. Gavin! I need to see my son. Please help me find him."

As we hurriedly walk down the hallway, I look at Mrs. Richardson with hesitation. I know there is something I need to talk with her about, and yet I just don't know how to approach the subject. After all, this is her son; what if I breach some kind of confidence or break some kind of trust?

"Mrs. Richardson, I know this is probably none of my business, but your son said something to me—actually, several things—that caused me to feel alarmed. When my wife and I found him at the side of the road, he made the comment that he didn't belong here. Any idea what he meant by that?"

"Maybe he meant that he didn't belong at the side of the road. I don't know. How am I supposed to know?"

Ed. D'Agostino

"No, I really think it is more than that," I respond. Immediately my mind goes back to the conversation at the side of the road. "He made comments to me such as, 'I'm not like them, I don't feel the same way, I don't live the same way, I don't believe the way they believe and because of those things, I don't belong.' Any idea what he may have meant by that?"

"I have no idea. He's a good kid, gets along with everybody. How am I supposed to know?"

"I believe he is a good and kind kid. He also said something about his secret getting out and that he shouldn't even be alive. Know what secret he might be talking about?"

"Look, I said I don't know and I don't. When we find him I'll ask him, okay?" Nancy says with annoyance.

"I'm sorry if I'm annoying you. That is not my intent. I'm just concerned about your son because he seems so upset."

"You'd be upset too if you were just beaten up."

"Yes, I'm sure I would be, but I really I think there's more to it than that."

"Look, I don't know what you're trying to get at here, but my focus is on finding my son. Are you going to help me with that or not?"

"I apologize; again, I didn't mean to upset you. Of course I'm going to help you. Where do you think he might be?"

"If I knew the answer to that question, I'd go there, but I have no idea, so let's just look everywhere, okay?"

"Okay, let's find him."

Going from room to room, my mind kept replaying the words "I shouldn't even be alive" over and over. What could Gavin mean by that? Why shouldn't he be alive? Doesn't everyone deserve a life?

CHAPTER 25

As I walk into the chapel looking for Gavin, I immediately see the young woman sitting there crying. How could I not? She is the only other living being in the room besides myself. Of course, my natural instinct takes over and I ask her, "What is the matter?"

She looks at me with eyes overwhelmed by grief and tells me about receiving the news from her husband's doctor that he is at the end of stage 4 liver cancer and there is only a short time left, maybe a few days at best. I am at a loss for words. Somehow, I know, in that moment, anything I say will have little or no meaning to her. Words won't comfort her. So, I mumble a feeble apology and sit down next to her. Just the idea that another human being is there to absorb some of her grief feels right.

As we sit there, her gentle sobs are the only sound in the room. And as I look around, that's when I notice them—a bouquet of flowers on the small table that is placed at the front of the room to serve as an altar.

"The flowers on the altar are beautiful, aren't they?" I ask her in some forlorn hope of getting her mind off of the news she has received about her husband.

Without looking up she replies, "Yeah, I guess they are. God, I'm going to miss him. What will I do without him?" she continues, never looking up.

"Were you married long?" I ask.

"A little less than five years," she replies. "What am I going to do? I feel so sad but I'm also so damn angry. God knows how much I love him, but boy can he get under my skin. I just don't know what I'm going to do."

"All marriages are like that, filled with moments of love and anger. I'm sure he knows how much you love him."

"I hope so. The last thing I said to him right before he slipped into the coma was how angry I was with him for getting sick. I yelled at him. He's lying there dying right in front of me, and I yell at him. What's the matter with me? I'm such an idiot. Oh God, what am I going to do now? I didn't even tell my dying husband I love him. It's funny how most people, myself included, say the hardest part of losing someone you love is finally letting them go, when actually the hardest part of all of this is coming to the realization you have to go on living without them being a part of your life. What am I going to do without him?"

"Funny thing about flowers," I continue as I once again look at the bouquet, "is when most people see a flower they only look at the colorful part and proclaim it to be beautiful and the only part that has value. But is that all there is to a flower? What about the stem? Every flower has a stem, doesn't it? Or what about the part of the flower that gives it life? The part that makes it possible for there to be a flower in the first place? What about the roots, the part that lives in filth, rot, and ugliness? Actually, the stem and roots are two of the most important parts of the flower, but do we proclaim them to be beautiful? No, they're 'ugly,' right? So, we cut the roots off, trim the stems and place them in a vase and look at our flowers, never acknowledging the stem and roots' existence, but they lived nonetheless. And because they lived, the flower had the opportunity to become what it has become, something beautiful and unique to behold. The beauty of which we remember long after it has gone," I say as a very personal memory of loss in my life suddenly engulfs me. "Well I've got to get going, I'm looking for someone. You take care of yourself," I continue as I stand to go.

The young woman looks up at me, gently places her hand on my arm and whispers, "Thank you."

I don't ask her what her name is, but I feel a bond has formed between us that makes knowing it irrelevant. And while knowing her name might make that bond stronger, because of being there for her in her moment of darkness I'd say it is unbreakable already.

As I walk toward the chapel door, I glance back at her one last time and I suddenly feel anger. Not at her, but at myself and society in general.

I'm angry that most people have this assumption they are going to live forever; I myself have felt this way. A further assumption is those whom one may find unacceptable have time to come to their senses and conform to the ways of life that "I" determine to be correct or noble or whatever.

But what do I do when the person I find so abhorrent and unacceptable dies before they come around to "my" way of thinking? My answer most likely will be something along the lines of, "Oh well, too bad so sad, I didn't know them anyway so who cares?"

By the same token, what if the person who dies is my child, spouse, or other relative or friend? Now how do I feel? Regretful, angry, ashamed, or still justified in my narrow-minded, condescending behavior? Or will I justify my grief by saying, "Well that's different, I knew them..." Question is, why does my not knowing someone make it okay not to care about them or grieve, in some form, over the loss of them?

Personally, I don't believe it is okay. Whether or not we know someone, they are still important to the overall fabric of every other life. When we take into consideration the many avenues each of our lives take, we come to realize how the vibrations of so many other people's lives, especially the stranger's, affect our own in numerous ways.

To that end I say, don't grieve for the person when they are gone, but grieve for yourself that you didn't get to know them when they were alive. Grieve for the missed opportunities to broaden your vision and deepen the level of your understanding by discovering the many nuances that make any and all societies unique and wonderful. Grieve for all of the times you simply dismissed another as irrelevant or worthless. Grieve for those things because we're the ones who have to live with ourselves. As a society of people known as the United States of America, we know what it is we need to do in order to evolve, grow, and become more united. We know the choices we have made in the past and are faced with making today that will effectively and successfully propel us into the future. And we must come to the place where it doesn't matter if those choices are hard or easy to make, because we know they must be made without complaint or fear.

Fortunes can be made, they can be lost, they can be made again, and they can be lost once more. Houses can be built, and they can just as easily be destroyed. Things, collections, items come into our lives in many different ways, but the thing is they can also slip right through our fingers. Regardless of if we like it or not, the fact of the matter is money, houses, and things are not constant, so in the end how much do they really matter?

Anyone with half a brain knows that things aren't permanent, and yet how many people live their entire lives pursuing them as if they are worth any and all sacrifice to obtain? To many people, all that matters is having a good paying job, a nice house or apartment, vacations, electronics, a big bank account, and so many other things that are actually transient. Most of us also have this mistaken belief that bad things only happen to others—never us. However, one day that just might change, and then what?

I was listening to the radio this morning and the song "You Matter to Me" from the Broadway musical *Waitress* came on and it gave me pause; I couldn't help but ask myself, what matters to me—and not just surface matters, but right to the bone matters? What causes me to fall into the abyss of feeling complete and utter loss?

Things can be replaced but people cannot. It doesn't matter how much money one has or how many properties a person owns; when someone leaves this life, no one (and let me emphasize that—*no one*) will be able to buy them back. They are gone forever.

Someone once said, "If we believe we are what we have and we end up losing everything and as such have nothing—who then are we?" While it is true there are many things that are necessary in order for our ultimate survival, are they really all that truly matter? Any storm can easily tear apart that which we see on the outside. In the blink of an eye, the wind will blow it all away, the rain will wash it all away, snow will bury it until it collapses, the earth will open up and swallow it, or fire will burn it beyond recognition. While it is true there are condolences and other expressions of sympathy for those who live through such a loss, why do we lose sight of the resolve they have? What about the hope and determination that lives deep inside of them, and actually, all of us? Without hope and determination, none of us would survive any of the storms that hit us daily. As such, we should not only focus on those things we think we have lost; rather, we cannot lose sight of what remains, because what remains is the only thing that really matters.

Who matters to you? Give them a real hug today! Reach out to them in some real way today! And today, let them know how much they mean to you. Because another fact remains—we don't know what the next moment, let alone what tomorrow, will bring. And anyone, and I mean anyone, who finds themselves reading this please know, you matter to me.

But does the stranger matter to me? To that I answer yes, because if we ever hope to move forward, we better get rid of this perception of us versus them. Someone once said, "I swore never to be silent whenever and wherever human beings endure suffering and humiliation. We must always take sides. Neutrality helps the oppressor, never the victim. Silence encourages the tormentor, never the tormented."

Why is it that we are put in the position where we feel we must take sides? There is this belief that it is us against them. But why? Where did it come from, and must it remain in order for any one of us to survive? Why is it okay to keep this idea alive? To me, it just seems so misguided and misleading. And yet to you, taking sides may seem like the most clear-headed and balanced thing to do in this diverse but uniquely beautiful society. But if that is your mindset let me ask you, how does taking sides really help or change anything? To me, taking sides only solidifies the justification to discriminate and as a further result, makes it feel more acceptable.

And while I agree there are times when taking sides is necessary, like standing beside someone in taking a stance against the oppressor or not remaining silent when others of the human race endure suffering because our silence only advances feelings of encouragement, taking sides just doesn't feel like the right next step. There is no room for the concept of understanding and acceptance to exist when human societies are fractured into sides.

The truth is, and we all know this because it definitely is a fact: we're all in this life together. The thing is, what we do with this fact determines how far forward as a civilization we will progress or how far backward we will regress. The choice is ours to make right now. Let's hope it's the right one.

And as you sit here reading this, you may think that you as one person could never make a difference, so who really cares what choice you make? Question is, what happens when everyone has the same mindset? Suddenly one voice has now become millions. And if it's okay for one person to have that thought, why isn't it okay for millions of people to have the same mindset?

"I wonder where Gavin could have gone?" I ask myself as I walk down the hall.

CHAPTER 26

Back in the emergency room, after finally finding three seats together, my wife is impatiently waiting her turn to have her cut looked at. "Where is that husband of mine and the kid we brought with us? I wonder if his parents ever found him? What happens if they call our number and those two aren't here? What am supposed to do then, just sit here and wait? Let someone else ahead of me? Good Lord, we'll be here all night if I let that happen and it's taking forever already," she mumbles to herself.

"Excuse me, are these three seats taken?" the stranger asks my wife.

"I was saving two of them for my husband and a boy we brought with us, but I don't know where they've gone to, so help yourself," my wife responds.

"Hi, my name is Michael, and this is my wife, Andrea, and our son, Tyler. We were caught in the shooting at Vinnie's Pizza."

"Oh my, yes we saw that on the television when we came here," my wife says. "What happened? Are you and your family okay?"

"It was actually horrible," Andrea replies. "One minute we were sitting eating pizza, and the next thing we hear are gunshots and people started screaming and running out of the place or hitting the floor. I don't think I'll ever forget it. I'll never stop hearing those gunshots and screams."

"It's okay, honey, we'll be fine. We'll see the doctor and then we'll head for home," Michael says to his wife.

"Any idea why it happened?" my wife asks.

"We don't know. Our goal was just to get out of there alive. Probably just some lunatic with nothing better to do," Andrea says.

"More likely some black guy or radical Muslim," Michael responds.

"God, Dad, do you always have to be so racist?" Tyler says to his father. "We have no idea who it was, but right away you're blaming it on a minority."

"According to the TV news they still haven't caught the guy," my wife says. "Was it just the one or were there more?"

"Could have been others but we only saw one; right, honey?" Michael says to his wife. "And he was wearing a mask."

"That's all I saw," Andrea adds.

"What's going on in the world? How often do we see this madness on the news or read about it?" my wife asks out loud. "And how long are we going to have to put up with it?"

"Some weirdo, that's for sure," Andrea replies.

All of them sit there for a few minutes, thinking their own thoughts as they watch all of the people around them.

"And how old are you, young man?" my wife asks Tyler.

"I'm eleven, ma'am," he replies.

"Eleven? You are becoming a young man. And what grade are you in, in school?" my wife asks the boy.

"Fifth," he replies.

"Do you like school? Do you have a girlfriend?" she continues.

"School's okay, I guess, and no I don't."

"That's all right, Son, your mother and I told you, you're too young to have a girlfriend," Tyler's dad says to him.

"I know what you're going to say, Dad, because if you've said it to me once, you've said it to me a thousand times: 'It's okay to have a girl as a friend but not as a girlfriend,'" Tyler says.

"That's right. There'll be plenty of time for you to have a girlfriend when you're older. Right now you're a kid, so enjoy it. It'll be gone before you know it," his father muses.

"Enjoy it? How am I supposed to do that?" Tyler asks.

"Hello all, may I sit here?" an old man asks. "It seems like I've been waitin' for hours, and I need to sit down for a bit. These old bones aren't what they used to be."

"That's all right, mister, you can have my seat," Tyler says to the stranger.

"By the way, my name's Robert," he says to the others sitting there.

The sad truth is Robert isn't long for this world. This is actually his tenth visit to the ER in as many days.

He is continually refused admittance to the hospital, not only because he lost his health insurance, but more likely because he has checked himself in so many times in the past. Every time he is given a clean bill of health and is released the next day. So, Robert is now considered nothing more than a hypochondriac who doesn't have anything wrong with him physically, or as the nurses and orderlies say about him, "He's nothin' but a crazy, lonely, old black man." However, even though he might be lonely, there is nothing crazy about him. Without any doubt in his mind, Robert knows the truth. How can he not know it? After all, he lives with it every day. He feels the pain and exhaustion. And what he feels is not just a result of growing old. There is more to it than that. Much more. Robert is dying and he knows it.

This is going to get good, my wife thinks to herself. *Especially after the conversation I've just had with these people, and now here's a black man who wants to sit with us. This should be interesting. Let's just see how much of God's love lives inside of them.* "Hello, Robert, my name is Ann," my wife says in return. "Sure, please sit with us." Turning to Michael and Andrea she continues, "You don't mind, do you?"

With some hesitation they respond, "Ah, no, that will be fine."

Looking at Robert, my wife asks, "Been waiting long?"

"About an hour or so, but like I said, it sure feels like about three or four hours. You?" Robert asks.

"About the same as you, maybe a little longer," my wife replies.

"A little longer. That seems about right. Why is it almost everythin' in life takes 'a little bit longer' to get here, or at least it feels like that? That is, until you know the end of your life is near and you only have 'a little bit longer' to live? How often have I heard the words—probably even said them myself—'it'll get better with time… give it a little longer, things'll change…' but nothin' ever seems to change; only gets worse. At least that's how it feels. 'A little longer' my ass. People think they have all the damn time in the world, but who knows for sure how much time any one of us has to live? What happens if waitin' 'a little bit longer' makes it all too late?" He pauses. "Sorry, went off there for a bit. But we were all given a voice and if I don't use mine, what do I have?"

"Seems like you're passionate about this time thing, Robert," Michael says. "Everything okay there? I'm sure Ann didn't mean to set you off."

"Again, I apologize, I'm sure she didn't. Just havin' a rough time of it, that's all."

"I guess we could say we all are. We were in the pizza place that got shot up tonight. I don't know if you've heard about that or not.

And this young lady is here because...actually, I'm not sure why she's here, she never said," Michael says, turning toward my wife.

"Oh, nothing as scary as what you've been through. I got a bad cut from a knife when I was doing the dishes. Like I said, nothing scary at all. And you, sir, what brings you to this God-forsaken place?" my wife asks Robert.

"Nothin' God-forsaken about it; it's here to help people like us who need help. I'm here 'cause I'm dyin'. That's why I went off like I did about time. Been dyin' for a while now, but no one seems to believe me, especially the doctors."

"If the doctors don't believe you, why are you here? Why come to an emergency room? Nothing but doctors and nurses here," my wife says.

"That may be so, but where else am I goin' to go? Besides, I'm still holdin' out hope they'll believe me one day, or at least before I die," Robert replies. "And if they don't, I'll know I did everythin' I could in this situation. Folks'll see I didn't just sit around talking a good game, but I actually did somethin' to try to fix it. I actually got in the game and did what I could."

Robert continues, "Terrible thing when people say they want things to be different but then don't do anythin' to make that happen. But I guess that's life and most folks seem to be happy with the way things are. Thing I don't get is, why are people okay with it? True, there are those that want to see things keep movin' forward, but then there are those who are more content in wantin' things to go backwards in time. How is that okay?"

"What are you talking about, Robert? When you say keep moving forward, what do you mean?" Michael asks.

"Like in my younger days, when the issues of equal rights for blacks was the thing. Sure, there were a bunch of people for it and there was another bunch of people who didn't want anythin' to do with it. Those folks would yell, 'Keep 'em seperated, put 'em at the back of the bus' or 'They can only sit at a certain place in the movies or at a restaurant.' But today it feels different."

"What makes it feel different?" my wife asks.

"We fought hard for our rights, lots of folks hurt and arrested, some even got killed to get us to where we are today, but now that we're here, instead of keepin' on goin' forward there's a bunch of folks that want to take us from today, when we actually feel like we are a part of society and have a chance of moving up and making things better for our lives, to a time and place when we didn't matter much. It's like some people, and from what I've seen they're mostly white folks, have no problem doin' away with the progress that we've made, includin' the government and other leaders. I just don't understand it and I guess I never will," Robert says. "I've been a church goin' man my whole life, and I remember readin' in the Bible how all of us are equal in God's eyes, so my question is, how does treatin' someone like they are less make them feel equal? And what does God think about that? Or how is it that if it says in one part of the Bible that in God's eyes we are all equal no matter who we are or how we live, but then in a different part it says that livin' that way is a sin; which one is right and which one is wrong? It's a contradiction, I'll tell you. I know it's got me confused."

"A sin is a behavior, an action, not a result of who we are or where we live," Michael replies. "Sin is a result of the choices we make. Nothing confusing about that."

"So, what you're sayin' is it's not a sin that I was born black and you were born white because we didn't have a choice?"

"That's correct, Robert," Andrea replies.

"Well then let me ask you somethin', if I didn't have a choice being born black and you didn't have a choice being born white and we're all equal in God's eyes, white or black because we were all created by God and in His image, how come white folks think it's okay to treat me, a black man, like I'm less important than they are? Same thing goes for everybody born in a different country in this world that God created and set up the boundaries on accordin' to Acts. If those people, whether they're Chinese or Vietnamese or whatever, didn't have a choice where they were born, what gives anyone else the right to condemn them or treat them as less than equal?"

And here we go, my wife thinks to herself. *I knew this was going to get good.*

"Are you sure God set the boundaries, or are they man made?" my wife asks, trying to keep things interesting.

"Like I said, it's right there in the Bible, Acts 17; you can look it up for yourself if you don't believe me," Robert replies.

"Oh no, we believe you, don't we?" my wife says, turning to the others sitting there.

No one answers.

"Well, is it all right to do that?" Robert persists.

"Do what?" Michael asks.

"Treat me as less than equal." Robert continues, "Actually, treat anybody as less than equal? Yeah, I can see if the person did somethin' terrible like killin' someone then they are treated differently, but how about those who are innocent and never did anythin' to anyone else in their life? Just because I'm an old black man doesn't make me not as good as a young white man, does it?"

"That's a good point, Robert. I actually believe that everyone is born equal and deserves to be treated the same way throughout life, no matter if they are black, white, or green or how old they are," Michael replies.

"Oh, do you now?" Robert asks.

"Yes, I do, don't I honey?" Michael says, looking at his wife. "I've always said that, haven't I?"

"You've always said that? Well those are just words if you don't back them up with actions. You know that, don't you?" Robert asks Michael.

"I think I've always acted in the best way possible to all people," Michael insists.

"Then why did you hesitate when I came over here and asked if it would be okay to sit down? And please don't tell me you didn't do that, I saw it with my own eyes," Robert says. "You and your wife stumbled around lookin' for the proper words and then you looked at each other before you said anythin'. Almost like you were lookin' for permission from each other. 'It's okay let the old black man sit down.' Why am I supposed to accept that? Why did it take your son, a boy, to offer me his seat? He didn't see me as a black man, but you and your wife sure did."

Again, no response from Michael or his wife.

"That is a good question, Dad," Tyler says, looking at his parents.

This just keeps getting better and better, my wife thinks to herself. *That's right Robert, challenge their narrow-mindedness.*

"Do you think the sayin's true, 'Makin' someone feel like less makes you feel like more'?" Robert asks no one in particular…

Is Robert right, do we judge others because we need someone to blame for our shortcomings, our self-imposed failures, our blindness to what true reality looks like? Do we simply dismiss others or judge them so that we can feel stronger and more self-assured?

Did you know that making another member of the same species feel inferior and keeping them down is a human behavior? Why do I say that? Just for a moment, think about the animal kingdom. Consider how many animals make each other feel inferior in any way. It doesn't happen. Does the African Bull elephant, which weighs an average of 14,000 pounds, make the 2 pound meerkat feel inferior? Do horses make goats feel inferior? Do cows make sheep feel inferior?

Even cats and dogs work together, which I know from first-hand experience. I'll never forget the day I came home and a dish of candy that was originally in the center of the dining room table was on the floor and the candy was completely eaten. There were candy wrappers everywhere. Now you might say the dog just grabbed a hold of the tablecloth and pulled on it until the candy dish fell; however, there was no tablecloth on the table. My wife only uses a tablecloth or table runner for special occasions.

"Well then, the dog must have jumped up until she reached the candy dish and pulled it down." While that might be the case for a larger breed of dog such as a Retriever or Shepherd, our dog was a Bassett Hound. So there goes that theory.

Actually, the only theory that is even remotely plausible is our cat jumped up on the table and nudged the candy dish over to the side of the table until it fell off. Our dog, which is one form of animal, somehow communicated to the cat, which is a different form of animal, her desire for the candy and even though they were different forms of animal, they were animals, nonetheless, who worked together to make that outcome real. And yet, how often do we use the expression "fighting like cats and dogs?" Did our dog and cat always get along? No, they didn't. Would it be safe to say our cat was bothered by the dog and vice versa? Yes it would be, and yet they overcame their differences and found a successful solution to achieve the desired outcomes. There were times they even played together and comforted each other.

Or how about plants? Oscar Wilde said, "A red rose is not selfish because it wants to be a red rose. It would be horribly selfish if it wanted all the other flowers in the garden to be both red and roses." Do flowers feel superior to each other in any way? Does a rose believe it is more beautiful than a daisy? Does an orchid feel it smells better than a lilac? Well that's just stupid, plants don't feel.

Albert Pine once said, "What we do for ourselves dies with us. What we do for others is and remains immortal." My question is, what about what we do to others? Does that remain immortal? How long do our words and actions against another stay with the person—a week, a month, a year, or longer? "You're stupid, you're fat, you're ugly, you're a no good..." How do we feel hearing words that describe us as inferior? How about the words, "You're smart, you're competent, you're the best, you're beautiful..." How does hearing those words make us feel? How do you think your words make others feel?

Yet why is it that we so vehemently hold onto those actions and words that undercut us to the point where we allow them to define our perceptions of how we see ourselves? Perceptions which we then translate into an assumed image of how society as a whole surely must see us: "The world definitely sees me the same way I see myself." And yet, look how we so readily forget the kind word spoken to us or helpful deed done for us, regardless if it is by an acquaintance or a stranger, that is, a different person, but a person nonetheless?

CHAPTER 27

"Did you find him yet?" Gavin's mom asks me as we meet in the hallway outside of the chapel.

"Not yet. Did you have any luck?" I ask in return.

"Oh God, where could he have gone to?" Mrs. Richardson asks no one in particular.

"Excuse me, may I help you?" the nurse asks us.

"I'm looking for my son," Nancy replies. "Actually, we're both looking for him, and we can't seem to find him. We've been all over this place. Can you help us?"

"I saw a young man, looked to be about fourteen, here about twenty minutes ago," the nurse replies. "I told him where the cafeteria is and he went there. Could that be him?"

"Oh, thank God! Where is it?" Nancy asks.

"Go down to the end of that hall there, turn left, go down that hall. You'll see a set of doors on your left. Go through them, down the steps, and turn right and you'll come right to it," the nurse answers.

"Thank you, thank you so much," I reply.

As we enter the cafeteria, I see Gavin sitting at a table by himself. He seems to be absorbed in thought and doesn't see us come in.

"Gavin! Gavin, I'm here," his mother yells as she runs to him.

"Mom, you're here!"

"Oh, my baby boy, are you all right? What happened? Look at your poor face. Why did you leave this man?"

"Is Dad with you? Where's Dad?" Gavin asks his mom.

"He's with this man's wife," she replies, pointing to me. "Come on, let's get you looked at. Are you okay?"

"Sorry I upset you, Gavin," I say to him as we walk out of the cafeteria.

"I thought I told you to leave me alone," Gavin replies, looking at me angrily.

"Gavin, what is the matter with you? This man is only trying to help you…"

The power of human empathy—leading to the collective action of helping others, including the stranger, actually frees us. Through empathy humanity can literally think themselves into another's place.

The sad thing is, how many of us, including you and me, choose to remain comfortably within the boundaries of our own experiences, never troubling to wonder how it would feel to be born other than "what we are?"

How many of us close our lives to those things that do not touch us personally, nor in any direct manner? How many choose to live in narrow-mindedness, narrow places, narrow confines where all might appear as understandable but are, in reality, places filled with misinformation and confusion?

How often are we afraid of losing ahold of that which we feel so strongly we control, that in the end we discover we have no real control over anything at all, and instead come to the realization it is because of our constantly living with the questions—what if, what if, what if—that the fear of the unknown has total and complete control over the life we profess to live so freely?

How many of us claim we are freed by pretense but are in fact enslaved to its mediocrity and as such are not free at all, but are instead merely playing some part on the stage of acceptance that has nothing whatsoever to do with who we are ultimately created to be?

"...Whatever, Mom."

"Not whatever, young man. What happened? Why were those boys beating you up?"

"I'm fine, Mom, don't worry about it."

"Don't worry about it? How can I not worry about it?" Gavin's mom asks him.

It was one thing to tell his mom not to worry about it, but Gavin's world was crumbling right before his eyes, so how was he supposed to not worry?

"Pastor Todd told me you said some pretty serious things to him when he and his wife found you. Is that true?" Nancy asks, looking at her son.

"I don't know? I probably said lots of things," Gavin replies. "What did he say I said?"

"He said you said you didn't belong because some secret was out. What secret and why don't you belong?"

Gavin feels nauseated. How is he going to explain this one to his mom?

"I probably said a bunch of stuff. But just because I said it doesn't mean I meant it," Gavin replies. "Remember, I was just beaten up."

"Why would someone beat you up?" his mother asks him again. "I just don't understand."

"I don't know. Geez, Mom, would you let it rest already? I'll figure it out."

"Figure what out? What's to figure out?" Gavin's mom continues.

"I don't know, Mom. Whatever." This is becoming a nightmare. All of the questions. When will they end?

As they entered the emergency room, Gavin's dad sees him and waves. "We're over here, Son," he calls to Gavin.

"Dad!" Gavin calls back.

As they hug Gavin's dad, visibly relieved, asks, "Are you all right, Son?"

"I'm fine Dad, or at least I will be physically."

"What happened? Why was someone beating you up?"

"It's a long story," Gavin answers. "I think you, Mom, and I need to talk."

"What's up, Son?"

CHAPTER 28

Several months later, my wife's cut is completely healed, but there is a deeper wound that I know needs to be attended to. And this is a wound that not only affects my wife, but me as well. That night finding Gavin and then sitting in the emergency room and then the hospital chapel with that young woman, all of it, stirred up memories that I thought I had successfully repressed. Now I see that any attempt to merely mask them in fake vibrato doesn't really address them or solve anything. Actually, what it does is makes them worse because I now see how I never confronted or accepted those thoughts and feelings and instead simply masked them in some feeble thought that I was moving on to some future success. However, I now realize that I need to be as brave as Gavin was that night and face it head on like he did when he told his parents his "dreadful" secret.

We all reach the end of our rope, or what some would call our breaking point; however, when we reach that point, is that really the end? Are we actually broken? Is that all that is left of life, or is there something else waiting for us around some unexplored corner? Are there still other choices that exist that are hidden behind this mask of what initially appears to us to be finality and brokenness?

The reality is, it is only when we reach the end that we can fully embrace the possibilities new beginnings present to us. Only when we are broken do we begin the process of repair.

And Lord knows I've been broken. I'll never forget that day as long as I live....

Dear Mom and Dad,

I don't know where to begin because I know you're hurting right now. I'm also figuring you're filled with a bunch of questions about why and how this could happen. Everything seemed so right and easy, but now it's so hard and you don't know why. Maybe I can help clear it up for you. Life isn't easy for you right now, I know. Well life hasn't been easy for me for years, only you never knew that 'cause I always had a smile on my face and made it all look good. But it really wasn't. For years I suffered in silence because I didn't know how to tell you what you now know. Call me chicken or scaredy cat or whatever but it's the truth, I was afraid. Afraid every day that I wouldn't be accepted and loved by the people who are supposed to love me the most, no matter what. Is it stupid to feel like that? Yeah, I guess it is but try to put yourself in my place hearing all of the negative stuff about other people. People that are supposed to matter and yet do they really? I mean, if you can be so unkind in your words and actions against each other, what's to stop you from being unkind to me? I guess that is what I am most afraid of. And you can say that it's different because I'm your child, but I'm still a human being with feelings and those feelings shouldn't only matter because I'm your child.

Do I expect you to understand? No, I don't, at least not right now. I do hope that one day you will understand how important words and actions are and will eventually find comfort and peace in knowing how awesome you both really are. I'll always

Ed. D'Agostino

cherish my childhood and the corny stuff we would do as a family. Riding my bike up and down the back alley or going to the park was always fun. You always took such good care of me when I was little, always making sure I had enough to eat and getting enough sleep. Reading me bedtime stories and making sure I had my little blanky to make me feel safe when I slept. But as I grew older, I knew deep down inside I was different. Did I choose to be different? No, but I am. I mean, who would choose to live without feeling accepted or belonging? I wanted more than anything to fit into your little world where all seemed safe and secure. Where everything looked normal and no one made waves or challenged the status quo. But I knew that would never happen. Like I said, I am who I am and no amount of wishing I was different is going to change that. So, I've come to the conclusion I have to accept myself for me. And even though I'm gay, I'm not some queer freakazoid. I'm a human being that just wants to feel love and acceptance like every other person. Question is, can other people, including you, accept me for who I am? My fear is the answer is no. And I just don't think I'm strong enough to accept that ultimate rejection. I know with Dad being in ministry how my lifestyle will affect all of that. People don't want a homo like me around. They made that clear in the anonymous letters you guys got. And I know I'm not supposed to know about them, but I do. And no, it doesn't matter how I found out, I just did. But really? Questioning what kind of parents you are? Really? You're great parents and you don't deserve that and I don't want to bring any more of it on you. So, I've decided to end the pain and confusion for all of us. Yes, I know there will be more pain for you at the beginning of this, but in time it will pass and I hope you come to see that this is all for the best.

I see how tired you both are and I'm tired too, so I think it's time we all finally get a break.

Never forget me and how much I love you. And sorry if I disappointed you.

And that was it. Our son was gone. The doctors told us the end of his life was painless and quick, but that information didn't bring much, if any, comfort because the question that was born out of that totally unjust and unacceptable loss remains to this day. For while it is true there is a large part of society which is unaccepting of others, especially the stranger, what about when someone is at home, including the child? Are they fully and completely safe there, or must they hide for some unfathomable reason and as such find themselves living on edge, even in the place where they should be able to feel the most secure and comfortable?

Is it because of the countless images and reports they are bombarded with daily that proclaim messages of "it's not safe out there for your kind, you're not welcome, you're not wanted"? And if they can't feel safe, welcome, or wanted by others of their own species, why should they feel safe anywhere?

And then my mind goes back to that emergency room before Gavin walked away...

"So, let me ask you Mr. Minister; if you've been discriminated against by the church and are made to feel like you don't belong, why stay there?" Gavin asked me.

"Where else would I go? The church has been my career for fifteen years," I replied.

"I don't know where you'd go, but what I do know is it's like you're all hell bent on making me see how I'm limiting my life by staying hidden behind my secret for fear I'll be discriminated against if it comes out. Well, I see it the same way with you. Aren't you limited because of discrimination? No, you may not be hiding from others, but are you really free to be who you are? How accepted are you by those who are supposed to be there for you, including the church? After all, isn't the church supposed to be open and welcoming to all?"

"No, I may not be accepted by everybody in the church, but I'm not supposed to put my full trust in them. My wife accepts me."

"Does she really? Because from where I sit, she doesn't seem too happy to me," Gavin observed.

"That's because of all of the baggage that comes with this job," I replied.

"But doesn't fully accepting someone mean fully accepting them no matter what they bring? I mean, how can someone say they accept someone if they don't take on everything that other person drags with them? And just because I don't like what they bring with them and feel like I can't accept it doesn't mean I don't have to respect it, does it? That's who that person is, because all of it is a part of that person's life story, and if I don't accept or respect another's life story, how can I ever fully accept and respect the person who lived that story? Actually, I can't. And that's what I'm most afraid of. Those closest to me, the ones who are supposed to love me no matter what won't accept or respect me once they know my secret. Question is, Mr. Minister, what are you afraid of?"

Boy, did Gavin's words open a wound. I mean, who are we to make another feel afraid of being who they are? Who are we to judge another for loving who they love or acting like they act? Just because they are different doesn't mean they aren't human and shouldn't be important. God, how easy it is to use someone and then just toss them aside like some piece of trash.

"Like I said, ministry has been my career for fifteen years," I replied, thinking I was dodging his question.

"Maybe, but is having a career the same thing as having a life?"

"No, a career is a job, and life is so much more than a job," I answered. "And I don't know what I'm afraid of."

"If the church has been your career for fifteen years, so what? It hasn't been your life, you just said so yourself. So, if having a career doesn't equal having a life, when do you go and live your life?" Gavin asked.

"I think we're getting a little off track here, Gavin," I said to him. "You're feeling like you do or don't belong has nothing to do with my job or career or anything like that," I continued.

"Doesn't it?" Gavin asked me.

"No," I replied.

"How come?"

"Because having a job and being true to yourself and allowing others to see who you really are are two entirely different things. Lots of people have been working the same jobs for years."

"That may be so, but did they live a life or just pay the bills to get by? Did you allow the people from the church to see you for who you and your family truly are?"

"What about the boys who beat you up?" I asked. "What are you going to do about them? You know who they are and if you let them get away with this, you're telling them that what they did was all right and that you deserved it. But did you deserve it?"

"No, I didn't deserve it."

"Then why not do anything about it?"

"Because if I do, look at what will happen to me. Not only will I be known as the faggot, but then I'd be known as the snitch too, and nobody wants to be a snitch. Did you stand up to those who discriminated against you? Or did you hide somewhere, just taking it?"

"As a matter of fact, I took the church to court. Earned me quite a reputation with the conference, let me tell you. Treated me like I was some kind of enigma."

"Didn't they treat you like that already when they discriminated against you?"

"Yeah, I guess they did, but I'm not sure I'm following your logic here, Gavin," I said in response.

"Well, it's like me with school; school is like my career and it is very important to me that I don't let the other kids really see who I am for fear they won't like what they see and I won't be accepted in my career as a student. So, the idea of me fitting in with the other kids in school is getting in the way of me being fully me and having the life I deserve to live. Same with you; you have a disability, but the church won't accept that, so you have to try to hide it or whatever. But by hiding it or brushing it off like it's no big deal and just accepting the discrimination is like denying a part of who you truly are. You can't be fully free in your life just so you can have a career. That's how it looks to me, but hey, I could be wrong," Gavin said.

Gavin's insight caused me to pause. Was he right? Was my career as a minister getting in the way of my life? Was it enhancing my life in any way, or was it filling it with pain and doubt? The church prides itself on doing so much good and it does in so many ways, but doesn't it also cause pain through judgmental attitudes and discriminatory actions? Lord knows how judged my family and I were by it. And the loss we suffered because of that judgment is irreversible.

"Let's say you're right about my career. Thing is, there is more to my story than you know," I said to Gavin.

"Like what?" Gavin asked. "You told me you'd share your story with me."

"We had a son."

"Where is he? What happened to him?" Gavin asked.

"It's a long story and you don't need to hear it," I replied.

"Why not?"

"Because it's personal and talking about it won't change anything anyway."

"How do you know?" Gavin asked.

"Because you're a kid and what insight would you have about it anyway?" I replied.

"Maybe because I'm a kid I have the best insight. The way you said you had a son, does that mean he's dead?"

"Yes, he's no longer with us."

"What happened? How did he die?"

"Like I said, it's a long story."

"But that story is a part of your life. If you're so hell bent on me sharing my story so I can fully live a complete life, why is it okay for you to devalue part of the story of your life? What is it? Are you ashamed of it or something?"

"No, I'm not ashamed of my story. I'm ashamed of myself," I replied angrily. "My stupid narrow-mindedness caused me to lose something I valued more than anything else." And then my mind once again drifted back five years earlier to the day before our son took his life...

CHAPTER 29

"I can get a job and help us out," my mother says to my father.

"How do you know what's going to happen out there?" Dad asks. "You're a housewife. It's a lot different out in the real world."

"The real world? Don't you think what I'm doing is important? Like my job taking care of all of us isn't real? Or don't you think it's a real job? Is that what you're saying, what I do isn't a real job?"

Here it comes again, another argument.

"No, that's not what I'm saying," my father replies. "All I'm saying is it's different. It's not easy to earn a paycheck, that's all."

"And what's so difficult about it?" Mom angrily asks in return.

"It's just different, okay?"

"And how is it different?" Mom continues.

"You need skills, experience, have to be fast on your feet and at times make quick decisions. Like I've said, it's different."

"I have experience. I have skills. I know what I'm doing," Mom says, her voice exposing her agitation. "And I'll have you know I make decisions all of the time."

"I'm sure you do, but deciding what to make for supper is a lot different than deciding which project is more important at work," my father counters. "I mean, just what kind of experience do you think you have to contribute to the world outside of this house anyway? And before you say anything, no, I don't think you're capable of making those kinds of decisions."

"Oh, really now?" From the tone of her voice I can tell Mom is getting madder by the second. "Well if you're so sure I'd never be able to contribute to the world, why don't we change places for a few days and see how you do? What do you think of that idea, huh?" my mother yells.

"Look I don't want to fight with you, okay? I just don't think you could handle it out there," my father says, pointing to the door. "And that's nothing against you, it's just the way it is."

"Just what year do you think we're living in?" Mom asks Dad. "It sure as hell isn't the fifties like you think it is."

"I know what year it is, and no, it's not the fifties. I just don't want to see you getting hurt by putting your name out there and getting rejected. Believe you me, I know how it feels, and I don't want you to feel the same way. What real work experience do you have to put on a resume anyway? You do know most places that are looking for workers want more than just an application, don't you? Besides, look at the world today, all of these accepting people, LGBTQ freaks, sodomites, terrorists, hatred, all of it. It may not have been better in the fifties but it sure felt safer and more innocent."

"You're a minister, you're supposed to be preaching about loving and accepting others, but listen to you. And how would you know what the fifties were like, you weren't even born until 1962. Besides, I have lots of stuff I could put on a resume."

"Oh yeah? Like what, doing the laundry, baking cakes? And maybe I didn't live in the fifties, but I heard about them from my parents and grandparents."

"No, lots of other things, like budgeting and things like that. You know, there's a lot more to running a house than just doing dishes and cleaning. There are a lot of things I can do. A lot," Mom says, her voice trailing off.

"Look I don't want to talk about this anymore. I'm hungry, what's for supper?" my dad asks.

Even though I can still see the spark of belief she has in herself, I can't help but wonder if she doubts herself anyway. I mean, Dad is a cool guy and all, but he's stuck in some kind of mindset from the past. Like it was better back then than it is today. And maybe in ways it was, but from what I've seen, it was pretty awful too. And if we only look at the good and ignore the bad, how will the bad ever get better? I mean they were pretty discriminatory back then against so many people, and not only because of color or religion, but even because of sex. And when you think about it, look how that discrimination held us back. Like with my mom. Who says my mom isn't as good as my dad? I think my mom is awesome, and she can do whatever she puts her mind to. And just because my dad says she can't doesn't mean it's true. Besides, who is he or anybody else to squash someone else's belief in him or herself? And what did he mean by LGBTQ and sodomites? He talks about them like they are some kind of freakazoids, but they're real people with real feelings—believe me, I know better than he does. I mean, what would he say if he found out his son is gay...?

Everyone wants closure, and discrimination is a form of that in many ways. Think about it; if I don't like someone or agree with things like their lifestyle, religious beliefs, nationality, politics, or even their sex, then I can openly discriminate against them, feel justified in my discrimination, and that's the end of it, case closed.

But is that really closure? Or is that just an illusion of closure that makes one feel free from all others? Because whether we like it or not, the reality of it is all others still exist.

When you think about it, how does someone move forward when it is apparent they aren't accepted by even their blood relatives? The evidence of this has been thrust upon them numerous times and in various ways that there can be no doubt that others hold more value to the concept of family than they do. And while it is true one can create a bridge as some sort of attempt to keep the family connected, what happens to the bridge when one side puts forth no real effort to maintain the structural integrity of their side of it and, as a result, one half of the bridge collapses? Or is the maintenance of the entire bridge the sole responsibility of the one who created it? For once that collapse has occurred, the bond has now been broken. As a result of that collapse, on one side of the bridge stands its creator looking forlornly at their half wondering what happened and how they can repair the other side of it in some way to have even the least bit of connection to those on the other side. Those on the other side continue on, never really noticing their half has collapsed because it wasn't really important to them in the first place. They may have said in words that it was, but their inaction in maintaining their half proves otherwise.

CHAPTER 30

At some point in my life I was told we are driven by six genetic needs: "Belonging, survival, love, power, freedom, and fun." Whether that is true for you or not I don't know, but what I have come to realize is how reality shows that belonging is the foundation of the other five needs. Without belonging they would be nothing more than nice ideas that sound good. Think about it this way for a moment: if we are cast out or deemed unworthy by those who feel they are "in the know" and as a result don't fully belong to all of society, our chances of survival dramatically decrease, we feel unloved, we have no power because no one respects or takes us seriously, and our freedom to be who we truly are is compromised. Additionally, how much fun is it to be alone?

But belonging can be a confusing word. On one hand it is defined as a possession, something owned as in, "It is one of their many belongings." On the other hand, belonging is defined as being accepted, being made to feel a part of, fitting in with.

Question is, are these different definitions of the word "belonging" tied together in any way? What I mean by this is, in order to belong to, as in being accepted by or fitting in with, must one first belong to (as in "owned by") another or group? In order to accept you, must he, she, it, or they feel like they own you first? Own you in the sense that you kowtow to their every whim, you sacrifice your true self to fit in, you disregard your own unhappiness because of not being accepted in order to make the unaccepting one feel good and content? In short, must you belong to them in order for you to belong with them? So, if one must be "owned" by someone in order to fit in, I guess the question then becomes: where in the end will that get them? Will they have sacrificed who they are, and the freedom to be who they are, in order for someone to have enough desire to want to "own" them so that they fit in?

What an interesting but complex concept to think about. But reality shows it to be true; take abstract art as an example. If I'm an art collector and I don't like abstract art—I don't understand it and in my opinion a child could do it—I would never accept it into my collection. Am I limiting myself because I am limiting my vision? And while I am not trying to discount anyone's opinion, because opinions are valid and real and as such must be respected, the question I need to ask myself is, is my rejection simply based upon an opinion that is formed from a misunderstanding? I don't understand abstract art, and as such, I don't accept it and would never own a piece of it? Pablo Picasso once said, "It took me four years to paint like Raphael and a lifetime to paint like a child."

Doesn't the same hold true for what are truly unimportant matters such as skin color, nation of birth, lifestyle, or religious belief? I don't understand any of those things and so I don't accept those who follow them?

I once saw an unattributed quote that read, "Truly loving another means letting go of all expectations. It means full acceptance, even celebration of another's personhood."

How often do we celebrate another's personhood? Actually, what the world needs is for every one of us to embrace who we are—celebrate it, live it fully, and let others see who we really are. Because once we celebrate who we are, we are then giving ourselves permission to celebrate who others are even if their lifestyle or agendas don't line up evenly with our own. Or as someone once said, "Let's practice what we preach, and with the acceptance that we expect from others, let's stop being so damn judgmental and crucifying everyone who doesn't fit into our boxed-in perception of what is right."

Don't ever let anyone tell you, "You don't belong." Don't ever allow yourself to believe just because you are not exactly like someone else then you are a worthless piece of garbage which can so easily be thrown away. Who misses a piece of garbage anyway? Just like who would miss those who are not like us? Nobody, right? Wrong!

The fact is, we need all others in order to survive. And we can vehemently deny that fact, but consider how many people of other races or beliefs or lifestyles help you on a daily basis? And if your first reaction is "none" then you need to ask yourself, "Who made the lunch I ordered, or designed the clothes I'm wearing, the car I'm driving, the cell phone I'm carrying, or filled the prescription I desperately need," and on and on and on? While it is true we need every one of those "strangers" to make our lives complete, look how easily we dismiss them because they aren't exactly like us or because they are poor or Democrat or Republican or gay or Muslim or whatever they are. We think we have the right to judge them in order to simply justify our narrow-minded dismissal of them.

And is our dismissal of others okay, or must we be better than having such an inferior mindset? Because what will ultimately happen if we hang on to an inferior mindset and continue to pull ourselves and others apart because of non-acceptance? I truly believe we will end up as nothing more than a fragmented society of selfish individuals. But is that what we want? Is that what we need? And you might be saying to yourself, "That's what we have already." And if you believe that to be true, then the question is, do we have to keep it that way or are there things we can do to help 'mend the wounds'?

Even though the earth is filled with people who are different, selfish individuals create a world that is like them and not like the one that literally surrounds them. They do this in order to safeguard themselves and protect their beliefs. Unfortunately when this happens, love and understanding between societies are replaced by stubbornness and unbending attitudes. Any door that may have had any chance of being open to possible change and growth has been slammed shut and tightly locked to keep out any and all "foreign invaders" that challenge us to look and think in ways that are contrary to our current mindsets and opinions.

If you want to be accepted for who you are, then you have to accept others for who they are. Instead of listening to the voices inside of your head, listen to the voice inside of your heart and ask yourself, "What is that voice telling me?" Is it telling me to throw away all of the Mexicans, is it telling me to throw away all of the Muslims and the gays and the lesbians or throw away the Bible-beaters? Just throw them away, get them out of your sight so you won't have to look at those worthless pieces of trash anymore? Is that what the voice in your heart is saying? I really doubt it.

Do we decide to not accept those who are different because they make us uncomfortable?

Well remember, as someone once said, "The first step toward change is awareness. The second step is acceptance."

Why shouldn't I talk to the stranger? What prevents me from saying hello, from reaching out in some way? Is it because the stranger doesn't say hi to me first? Is it because they ignore me? Do we already have too much on our minds to care? That's how it seems. Just these two vessels cloaked in skin walking past each other without even seeming to notice or care about each other. Just these two vessels that will die in some measure of loneliness if some type of bond is not formed between them.

Yet what's really amazing to me, and I'm not sure if you are aware of this or not, is how if we don't fully accept ourselves, the stranger we so easily ignore actually lives inside of us. And a further irony of it is we nurture that stranger. Think about it. We feed the stranger that lives inside each of us whenever we feed ourselves. We take care of the same said stranger inside of us when we are sick. We try to fulfill the stranger's desires, because the reality is they are our desires too. And if that stranger somehow attains some level of success, without hesitation we join in the celebration. And we also cry right along with that stranger when they fail. Yet how many of us realize this? My guess is not too many.

And I know other questions exist such as, "Why do I have to accept, let alone love, somebody who I don't agree with, someone I don't even know or makes me uncomfortable? Why and how am I supposed to do that? Why should I love the homo or the libtard or the repukelicon or the...?"

I guess it all depends upon your definition of love. How expansive or restrictive is it? Does your definition of love only include those you know or are related to? Does your definition of love only include your closest circle of friends and family, and all others who may find themselves outside of the circle are not worthy of being accepted, let alone loved? The only thing they are worthy of is judgment and exclusion? Or does your definition leave room for at least the possibility of loving all others, including those you may not know or agree with? And which definition would lead to the better way? Every one of us is faced with making choices countless times every day, and while it is true our individual histories do play a role in guiding us in the choices we make, we cannot and must not use our history as some sort of crutch thinking that it will support any and all excuses we make to justify our choices.

After taking into consideration all that we have faced and conquered, my wife and I decide we are more than the sum total of a bunch of temporary items that won't last forever. And now at this new stage of the journey, I've discovered getting rid of possessions has shown me that I am still me. I am not defined by what I own or think I have lost, but by who I am at this very moment, and what I do to better myself for the next. And it is the same with all of us. However, if we merely settle for the things in life that we feel will finally set us free, like lots of money or houses, clothes, or other possessions, what will we have ultimately settled for?

I have also come to the realization that my life must change, because if nothing ever changes there will be no sunrise the next morning. Everything we see or own can be replaced. Everything except the person or people that surround us. Once they are gone, they are gone forever. And while it's true their memory may live on in us, there is still this void that cannot be filled because of their absence. Mary Catherine Bateson said, "The timing of death, like the ending of a story, gives a changed meaning to what preceded it." What has preceded the time you now find yourself living in? And would the death of another change the meaning of it in any way? After taking my son's brief life into consideration, I now realize mine has got to change in many ways if I ever hope to fully live it.

To hell with living a mediocre life. To hell with living a life where you denounce and criticize who others really are so that you can feel important or safe because you think you need to fit in with some narrow confines of acceptance as defined by those whom you deem to be in the know. I've lived that life. I've traveled that road. I've tasted discrimination and I've discriminated against others and quite frankly I'm tired of all of it. Nelson Mandela said, "There is no passion to be found in playing small and settling for a life that is less than the one you are capable of living."

For too many years I have spent my life living among the enemy. The enemy being those who pass judgment upon me and my family. Those who decide it is easier and better for themselves to denounce and devalue that which is precious to me. But because of what has happened and what continues to happen, and not only in my life but in the lives of so many others, I have decided it is time to change what can appear to be an inevitable and unyielding fact. The time has come to surround myself with those who unwaveringly accept all others. Because for me, or any one of us, to settle for anything less is truly tragic.

In order to move forward, you must be present in heart, mind, body, and deed in the very moment in which you find yourself living. You don't merely belong to the past and what came before, just as you cannot only belong to some mindset of what the future might be—rather, you belong now. Actually, this holds true for all of us.

Use the lessons from the past to help you succeed now. Relish your dreams of the future and allow the hope of them to give you the strength you need to overcome any obstacles that will surely present themselves on your journey of life. But do not allow those lessons and dreams to confine your possibilities to some narrow corridor that is unbending, blinding and disbelieving. Think of a corridor—it only allows one way in and one way out. Do you really want to live your entire life in a corridor?

Six months later as I finish packing the car with the few necessities my wife and I have decided to take with us, the question comes to me…Who does anyone truly belong to? Sure, we can say family, spouse, and other loved ones, but is that the case in every instance? Actually, thinking about it, the only person we truly belong to is ourselves. I think once we realize that, we can find the freedom we so desperately need to finally and fully accept all others and make them feel like they belong too.

"Okay, dear, are we ready to go?" I ask my wife.

"Yes, let's go," she replies.

"Remember that kid Gavin we found at the side of the road? I wonder what ever happened to him?" I ask.

"What made you think of him?" my wife asks me in return.

"I don't know. He just popped into my head," I reply.

"Probably off somewhere living his life," my wife says.

"You're probably right. Time to start living ours," I reply.

As I back out of the driveway, the journey to this new and unknown place across the country seems less frightening and more hope-filled than any journey of life I have ever taken. I wonder if it's because I finally feel like I belong? And as I turn on the radio, guess what song is playing?

A final thought or two

According to Zig Ziglar, "Repetition is the mother of learning, the father of action, which makes it the architect of accomplishment." As you read through this discourse, I wouldn't be surprised if there were times when it felt redundant to you. "Okay, I've read about that before, okay you've said that already, okay I get it, enough already..." If you have any of those thoughts, the truth is I set this book up that way for a specific reason. My intention was to reinforce in all of our minds the importance of others, including the stranger.

Further, while I know there were numerous questions asked throughout this book, you probably feel like they weren't fully answered. Well you, the one reading them, are ultimately responsible for answering those questions and not only in ways that make you feel comfortable, but more importantly, in ways that challenge you to become that person that looks at another and sees something amazing. Because if I simply give you the answers to all the questions asked throughout these pages, all you will end up with are a bunch of someone else's opinions, and how much will your love grow from that?

About the Author

You belong right here, right now. While you may have trouble believing that, Ed. D'Agostino doesn't. As a result of suffering from epilepsy, Ed. knows what it feels like not to belong, as well as the adverse effects of discrimination. In addition, his fifteen years of working in ministry and ministerial counseling have shown Ed. the many nuances that not being accepted takes in people's lives and the wounds it causes. He is currently working on his second novel titled *Back Booth*. It is the story of a man who finds renewed hope in the face of seemingly overwhelming adversity. Ed. currently lives in Dunedin, FL with his wife Michelle and his daughter Emily. Ed. enjoys reading, nature, and the arts.